THE ROWMAN & LITTLEFIELD GUIDE TO WRITING WITH SOURCES

THE ROWMAN & LITTLEFIELD GUIDE TO WRITING WITH SOURCES

FOURTH EDITION

JAMES P. DAVIS

ROWMAN & LITTLEFIELD PUBLISHERS, INC.
Lanham • Boulder • New York • Toronto • Plymouth, UK

10/13   6/12   2 TC
LAD

5/19
LAB
TC

Published by Rowman & Littlefield Publishers, Inc.
A wholly owned subsidiary of
The Rowman & Littlefield Publishing Group, Inc.
4501 Forbes Boulevard, Suite 200, Lanham, Maryland 20706
http://www.rowmanlittlefield.com

Estover Road, Plymouth PL6 7PY, United Kingdom

Copyright © 2012 by Rowman & Littlefield Publishers, Inc.

The lines from "Diving into the Wreck". Copyright © 2002 by Adrienne Rich. Copyright © 1973 by W. W. Norton & Company, Inc, from THE FACT OF A DOORFRAME: SELECTED POEMS 1950-2001 by Adrienne Rich. Used by permission of the author and W. W. Norton & Company, Inc.

British Library Cataloguing in Publication Information Available

Library of Congress Cataloging-in-Publication Data

Davis, James P., 1954-
  The Rowman & Littlefield guide to writing with sources / James P. Davis. — 4th ed.
      p. cm.
  Includes bibliographical references and index.
  ISBN 978-1-4422-0569-7 (pbk. : alk. paper) — ISBN 978-1-4422-0570-3 (electronic)
  1. English language—Rhetoric—Handbooks, manuals, etc. 2. Research—Methodology—Handbooks, manuals, etc. 3. Report writing—Handbooks, manuals, etc. I. Title.
  PE1478.D37 2012
  808'.0042072—dc23

                                                              2011042196

Printed in the United States of America.

For R. Baird Shuman,

for whom kindness, integrity, and
teaching have always been synonyms

CONTENTS

A NOTE ON
THE NEW EDITION

The first editions of *The Rowman and Littlefield Guide to Writing with Sources* emphasized the persuasive power, authority, and confidence that writers gain by learning to place their ideas into written dialogue with published information and opinions. Those editions focused on choosing, assessing, integrating, and citing that material with clarity, efficiency, and grace as indispensable skills for a writer of nonfiction. I'm preserving both that emphasis and what I'm hoping is an optimistic tone in this fourth version of the book. Reading critically—being alert to relationships among ideas and authors' positions and alert to how other authors use and present information—does not merely give one the substance for an essay and connect one's text to the actual world. And learning to use such material responsibly and to cite it clearly is not merely a matter of pleasing teachers and editors, who are ever more alert to the ethical and legal consequences of plagiarism. Approaching published and electronic sources of information with a mix of enthusiasm, mature skepticism, and confidence enables writers to discover and refine their own ideas and to express them with an emphatic and vigorous voice.

For this edition, I am indebted to James Weaver, whose sharp editorial eye spared me much embarrassment.

THE CHALLENGES OF ACADEMIC WRITING IN THE AGE OF MISINFORMATION

The purpose of this book is to enable you to write with confidence and authority so that your readers will trust what you say and value your viewpoint. As sources of information multiply and compete for attention, and as readers grow increasingly skeptical of such information, you need to earn your readers' attention as well as their trust. Busy and distracted people in a media-rich culture have little patience for sloppy work when deciding what to read. You can increase your chances of engaging them as readers if you demonstrate your care as a writer and show your awareness of their needs as readers, your knowledge of the topic, and your responsibility in using credible sources of information in reasonable ways. Finding credible sources might seem to be a difficult challenge at a time that has been called the "Age of Misinformation" (Stelter). Unfortunately, that label is more than an amusing reference to the more common phrase "Information Age."

The problem is not that we are lacking reputable sources of information or that our interest in them is waning. According to Andrea Foster, by 2007, the Web had more than 100 million sites, and the number of online scholarly databases had grown to over 18,000. "Students are drowning in information," Foster adds. Demand for nonfiction has never been greater. According to a researcher at the University of California, San Diego, we consume "triple the amount of 'content' that we consumed in 1980" (Falk). Nonfiction books and memoirs are enjoying robust sales. Nonfiction documentary films are getting widespread release at neighborhood cineplexes, and nothing boosts a movie's popularity quite like the claim that it is based on a real story or inspired by real events. News programs are proliferating throughout network and cable television, and some of the most popular prime-time shows are reality based. The market reveals that the public has an appetite for truth, reality, nonfiction—whatever we choose to call it. Yet much of what passes for truth is clearly something else—doublespeak, propaganda, plagiarism, advertising, public relations, fraud, or spin. These are times that require readers to be skeptical or, better yet, cautious and responsible.

The unreliability of much that passes for truth has itself become a major topic in the media. Pundits, talk-show hosts, journalists, and comedians regularly discuss and argue about news coverage. What gets discussed and how it is presented are themselves newsworthy and controversial subjects. While the discussion has the potential to encourage viewers and readers to be more thoughtful and critical about information, the dialogue about information sources has been subsumed into broader culture wars. CNN's weekly program *Reliable Sources*, a round-table discussion of the news media by print, broadcast, and online journalists, is matched by Fox News Channel's *Fox News Watch*, which brings two conservatives and two liberals to a panel discussion of the week's leading stories. Nonprofit media-watch organizations face off in accusations of bias on the right and on the left. Fairess and Accuracy in Reporting (FAIR) documents the media's glect and misrepresentation of issues construed as liberal; the dia Research Center calls itself "America's Media Watchdog" and alerts its members to what it presents as leftist bias in the products of the major news organizations.

Beyond issues of bias and slant, the debates increasingly concern disagreements about literal facts. In *True Enough: Learning to Live in a Post-Fact Society*, Farhad Manjoo examines what he calls "the creeping partisanship" that "has begun to distort our very perceptions about what is 'real' and what isn't": "No longer are we merely holding opinions different from one another; we're also holding different facts. Increasingly, our arguments aren't over what we *should* be doing—in the Iraq War, in the war on terrorism, on global warming, or about any number of controversial subjects—but instead over what is *happening*" (2). In his 2010 commencement speech, the president of Muhlenberg College, Peyton Helm, described the problem as one resulting from our "à la carte society": "We each have our own playlists and our own headsets. . . . We need not watch anything we're not interested in, nor listen to anything we disagree with, nor to anyone who might challenge our assumptions and make us think" ("On Compromise"). The not-very-distinguished media debates about whether Saddam Hussein was involved in the attacks on 9/11, or if President Obama was born in the United States, or whether human activity has contributed to global climate change—such politically charged issues illustrate well how "facts" can be hand-selected and even fabricated to further an agenda. If there is a consensus about civic issues and the media, it is that most of us use the media to find the set of "facts" that will confirm what we already believe to be true, to reinforce rather than overcome our prejudices.

QUESTIONS OF AUTHORSHIP AND AUTHORITY

If political and cultural biases have contaminated the reliability of sources that claim to be balanced, fair, or objective, so too have questions and doubts about authorship raised their own sorts of problems. When one's actual identity can be so easily masked and when the openness of the new media permits free access and unrestricted posting of viewpoints, the process of reading becomes fraught with complications. The online encyclopedia *Wikipedia* relies on the public's ability to revise its entries, on the theory that errors will be corrected and simplistic claims will become more nuanced. But when the veil of anonymity is lifted (by such sites as *WikiScanner*), many of the contributors or editors are revealed to be motivated less by truth than by public relations. If readers rely on *Wikipedia* and believe it without question, they might be deprived information about such things as the health effects of drinking Pepsi; or the severity of the Exxon oil spill in Port Valdez, Alaska; or differences of opinion about Walmart's pay to its employees; or criticism of Diebold voting machines (Hafner). Despite good-faith efforts of *Wikipedia* to monitor and protect its site, the popularity of the resource makes it particularly vulnerable to the suppression of information or the invention of damaging viewpoints by individuals or groups bent on sabotage.

The electronic media make it easy to disguise the identity of the authors of material. For example, some elected officials pay staff members to ghostwrite Twitter messages for them, creating the impression that they are in constant contact with the voters (F. Rich). Websites might have appealing and idealistic names but might actually be masking the corporate or public relations identity of the authors. One organization that tracks such websites is the Center for Media and Democracy (CMD), which publishes *SourceWatch*, described as a "collaborative, specialized encyclopedia" that "profiles the activities of front groups, PR spinners, industry-friendly experts, industry-funded organizations, and think tanks trying to manipulate public opinion on behalf of corporations or government." CMD calls websites published by such groups "astroturf" because they masquerade as locally managed citizens' groups (called grassroots political movements) but are actually written and funded by corporations or larger-scale political groups. CMD explains,

> Unlike genuine grassroots activism which tends to be money-poor but people-rich, astroturf campaigns are typically people-poor but cash-rich. Funded heavily by corporate largesse, they use sophisticated computer databases, telephone banks and hired organizers to rope less-informed activists into sending letters to their elected officials or engaging in other actions that create the appearance of grassroots support for their client's cause.
>
> ("Astroturf")

The organizations behind such websites are typically nonprofit organizations whose chief sources of funding are for-profit companies. The public relations arms of corporations realize that readers are often skeptical of websites with .com domains, which signify that their chief purpose is commerce. Forming a nonprofit organization not only masks their actual identity with an idealistic sounding name but also qualifies them for the .org domain.

Information found on an astroturf website can be useful in representing a particular group's perspective, but you should be aware of ways that the content is slanted to support the particular financial and political interests of those who fund the organization. *SourceWatch* discusses many such organizations, including Citizens for Cable Choice (opposing regulation of the cable TV industry), the Center for Consumer Freedom (promoting the interests of tobacco, alcohol, and food manufacturing companies), the Global Climate Information Project (a front for American automobile manufacturers), the Foundation for Clean Air Progress (run by the American Petroleum Institute), the Health Benefits Coalition (a group of insurance companies and health-care providers), Public

Interest Watch (heavily funded by Exxon Mobil), and some 200 others. Unless we understand how an organization is funded and whose interest it serves, we are likely to feel cozy and reassured by such words and phrases as *choice, freedom, progress,* and *public interest.* Such organizations regularly pick and choose the information they provide and slant its presentation in ways that enable industry advocates and lobbyists to argue in opposition to legislation or regulations that they perceive as threatening. The sources for such information are often deliberately obscured, as are the actual interests being represented on the websites. The increasingly complex ways that for-profit and nonprofit organizations are becoming entangled make it crucial for readers to proceed with caution and skill when searching the Internet for information on controversial topics.

Questions about the authorship of information are not limited to online sources. Consumer publications present a similar challenge. The economic pressures placed on magazines and newspapers have made them increasingly friendly toward major advertisers and open to printing material that does not originate with journalists. Magazines, critics claim, are under the corporate thumb of advertisers who demand "complementary copy" and "advertorials" before they provide the essential funding for the publications. When corporate sponsors demand an "ad-friendly" environment or, worse, when they rule out coverage of controversial topics in any issue they fund, then the publications become means of recruiting consumers for advertisers instead of reliable sources of information (Baker). With the layoff of thousands of reporters and the closing of major news bureaus, newspapers have been publishing fewer stories and have represented items written by others as original material. According to John Sullivan in "True Enough: The Second Age of PR," "even original reporting often [bears] the fingerprints of government and private public relations." Discussing a Pew Center study of the reporting on six major subjects by the *Baltimore Sun* in 2009, Sullivan notes that "63 percent of the news about those subjects was generated by the government, 23 percent came from interest groups or public relations, and 14 percent started with reporters" (37). These numbers do not necessarily mean that the information in these articles was false but that the authors of the pieces were not always reporters and that their content was not generated in accord with journalistic standards.

Comedians and self-described "fake news" programs have flourished in this cultural environment, as the outright silliness and deception of much of the media provide a constant supply of material. Underlying such comedy programs as Jon Stewart's *Daily Show* and Stephen Colbert's *Colbert Report* is some serious media criticism. The satiric vocabulary invented to mock shoddy reporting and misleading arguments reveals much about the state of the current media. During the premiere segment of Comedy Central's *Colbert Report*, Colbert introduced the word *truthiness* to describe a claim or position expressed with seeming certainty that is based not on evidence but on little more than the desire for it to be true. At a time when even scientific claims about stem cell research and cold nuclear fusion have been found to be hoaxes, *truthiness* seems to characterize the times. The American Dialect Society chose *truthiness* as the 2005 Word of the Year. The Merriam-Webster online community designated it as Word of the Year for 2006. As a commentary on *Wikipedia* and other reader-edited resources, Colbert introduced the word *wikiality* to mean reality as determined by majority rule, things treated as fact only because they are widely held assumptions about what is real. In "Truth: Can You Handle It?" Monica Hesse reports that a wiki-weather site, *Cumul.us*, enables its readers "to collaboratively decide whether it is raining outside," and *UrbanDictionary* now lists "collateral misinformation" as the deliberate changing of a *Wikipedia* article so that a person can win an argument. In a tribute to Colbert, Charles Seife titled his book *Proofiness*, which details the ways in which an erroneous claim can be made to seem true if it employs numbers to give it seeming authenticity. As one reviewer of the book puts it, "people fudge with numbers, sometimes just to sell more moisturizer but also to ruin our economy, rig our elections, convict the innocent and undercount the needy. Many of [Seife's] stories would be darkly funny if they weren't so infuriating" (Strogatz). There is a comic side to truthiness, astroturf, and proofiness, but the consequences of misinformation are serious. When people read only the things that confirm what they already believe and when groups are attempting to reason from contradictory sets of "facts," then the difference of opinion between groups who disagree becomes exaggerated, conversation devolves into shouting, and distrust has the potential to become hatred.

EVALUATING SOURCES AND ENTERING THE DIALOGUE

Writing during such times requires extra diligence about what and how you read and how you represent information to your reader. If the Internet and the newsstands seem to be filled only with advertising, half-truths, and shabby information, you might feel that there is little point to reading and research—as if it is all lies anyway. That attitude is what some people call "hyperskepticism," the unwillingness to believe anything, to see anything as credible, or to discern the difference between reliable information and deception. Surrendering to that kind of frustration, however, will diminish your authority and confidence as a writer. Instead, you should learn how to find, assess, use, and cite sources relevant to your study. Putting your ideas in dialogue with those of other writers creates an indispensable context for your discussion, adds to your readers' trust of your work, and broadens the significance of what you say.

When evaluating any source, you should be conscious of what professional standards govern its medium of publication. The standards for Internet sources are wide open, so assessing websites requires special care. The relatively stable domain suffix names, such as .com, .org, .net, and .edu, are changing as of 2012, but even now they are too blunt an instrument to be of much use in determining the reliability of a site. A .edu domain could be a university's archive, a professor's material for her class, or a student's project. A .com domain typically signals a corporate owner with a profit motive, but it is also the domain for major news organizations, whose reputation and journalistic standards assure a certain minimum of credibility. When you find something useful on a website, look for signals that the site is maintained with a sense of responsibility:

- transparency about who produces the site
- contact information and credentials for the person responsible for the site
- posted dates of most recent revisions
- clearly cited sources for information
- other signs that the site is maintained with currency and care (such as links that work properly)

Sites that are produced by reputable organizations and ones that are online venues for established print publications will be more polished and trustworthy than personal blogs or sites with vague authorship. Remember that your computer (or the library's computer) gives you access to some scholarly databases that are far more reputable than most actual Internet sites. These databases present searchable archives of publications and documents. Some of the databases, such as *LexisNexis* or *ProQuest*, permit you to restrict your search results to scholarly or research articles. Newspapers and popular consumer news magazines, whether in hard copy or in an online archive, presumably adhere to rigorous journalistic standards, but many shape their stories to serve an ideological stance or to please advertisers and other constituents. Further, as Arthur S. Brisbane (public editor of the *New York Times*) explains, "The rules of attribution and credit in the domain of scholarship are established, strict and well-understood. Journalism, by contrast, lacks a formal code for citing scholarly work." If you are writing for a college class assignment, the nature of that assignment and of the topic as you shape it will determine whether Internet sources and the popular or commercial press are likely to present relevant or adequate information. If you are writing about public opinion of a topic (as opposed to discernable facts about it), then samples of that opinion are what you need. Any number of websites will provide representations of information, complete with rhetoric, opinion, bias, and purposeful misrepresentations. Whatever your topic, however, you should learn how to assess the kind of source you have found so you may represent it accurately in your own work.

Most of the writing you complete for college and graduate courses will probably be informed by scholarly or academic sources—the most rigorously monitored and, we hope, most reliable information. A scholarly source is one that is peer reviewed or produced by a journal or university press. A scholarly article undergoing the process of peer review has been sent by the editor to other scholars with the same area of expertise to get their evaluation of the quality of the work, its significance, relevance, and appropriateness for the journal or press that is considering publishing it. Working independently of one another, usually without knowing the identity of the author, this impartial group of scholars offers a much more rigorous assessment of the work than that conducted by the editors of popular consumer magazines. To find such publications, also called "refereed" works, you can consult major bibliographic resources in your field, limit your online searches to peer-reviewed works only, work with a reference librarian, or look up a particular title or press in *Ulrich's Periodical Directory Online*. Notably, when you are looking at a scholarly publication, you will notice the systematic and careful way in which all sources of information have been cited in the work and listed in a bibliography. It will also be crucial for you as a writer joining the written conversation on a topic to be as systematic and careful in noting the works you have used.

We hope that colleges and universities are havens of clarity, integrity, and critical thinking—where standards of reasonable argumentation and ethics guide communities of teachers and students as they test ideas and learn to reach valid conclusions. Of course, colleges have that potential and sometimes attain it. But they haven't been immune to sloppiness and deceit, as we're reminded whenever we read of a college president, dean, or professor who has been accused of plagiarism. In a graduate program at a large university, more than three dozen current and former students have been accused of plagiarizing in their master's theses (Gray). A national organization, the Center for Academic Integrity, found in its most recent surveys that "22 percent of students say they have cheated on a test or exam, but about twice as many—43 percent—have engaged in 'unauthorized collaboration' on homework" (Young). Called a plague of plagiarism, this widespread academic dishonesty has been blamed on such things as the ease of cutting and pasting from the Internet or even on habits of intellectual theft encouraged by free music downloading on websites like Napster. It's likely that the continual invention of new technologies and types of sources has left students (and even some of their teachers) confused about how to assess, select, and use both published and electronic information.

Given the challenges posed by abundant material of questionable reliability, it's doubly important that you learn how to make the complex choices involved when you're reading, researching, and writing. Reading with a critical eye involves essential intellectual skills, as you assess the relationship of the information you have found to your project, evaluate its credibility and relevance, select the best use of the material, represent it accurately and fairly, and fully and coherently integrate it into your project. You must also acknowledge and cite the sources you have used in a methodical and clear way. Whether you quote them or paraphrase the information you have found; whether they are published books, unsigned articles, or documents found on the Internet; and whether your project is a formal report, a personal essay, or an oral report in a seminar, you must clearly signal that you have employed these resources and learn to cite them in ways that are ethical, precise, rhetorically effective, and consistent with practices established for the field in which you are writing. Learning to read critically and to write responsibly is crucial—not merely to staying out of trouble but to making sense of one's position during a time of truthiness. Consistently practicing the skills discussed in this book will help you to detect misuse of information by others and to write with more confidence and clearer purpose yourself.

DECISIONS TO MAKE

When you wish to use some information you've found or to quote a viewpoint that is expressed in some source, you need to make a number of decisions.

- Do you need to acknowledge the source of your information?

- Should you paraphrase or quote the material?
- If you are quoting, how much of the passage should you reproduce in your paper?
- How should you introduce and present the material?
- How should you make the transition to the quoted material and then back to your own prose so that your readers will always understand the status of the words they are reading?
- How should you cite electronic and Internet sources?

This book will help you to answer these questions.

PLAGIARISM

The writing skills involved in using quotations or information from sources are basic ones that you must employ in *all* of your writing. Your ability to use sources ethically and clearly is crucial to your success in every course, in any major you pursue, in whatever profession you choose. Yet college students often lack these basic skills. The purpose of this book is to enable you to incorporate quoted or paraphrased material into your writing in ways that credit the sources you consult for wording or ideas that are not your own and that will permit your audience to comprehend your ideas and to have confidence in your authority as a writer. Mastering the skills discussed here will broaden your options as you write, increase your confidence as a student, and empower you to write with clarity and authority. Neglecting these skills will hinder your abilities to communicate and, worse, in some cases, render you vulnerable to charges of academic dishonesty.

Very few students plan to cheat when they begin a course or when they begin a specific project. Most cases of academic dishonesty arise from poor planning, procrastination, carelessness, or intrusions of stress into students' lives that they haven't learned to manage. As a deadline approaches, students might be tempted to lift ideas or phrases from someone else's work. Or, in a rush to complete a project, they might allow themselves to take such sloppy notes that they can no longer tell what is their phrasing or what is someone else's or which source might have provided something that is scrawled in their notebook. In an English class, they might feel they can use unacknowledged ideas from *CliffsNotes* or *SparkNotes*. Students usually realize that these are such undistinguished study guides that they don't want to disclose they've consulted them—but some of the wording or an occasional idea might seem too good not to use in an essay. Even if students don't think they are doing wrong, even if the idea or phrase trickled into their work through carelessness or haste, these violations are taken as seriously as if students copied someone else's lab report or put their name on an essay written by someone else. You shouldn't consult a source that you would be ashamed to cite. If you ever have a question about the way you are completing an assignment, ask your professor or lab assistant how to proceed. For example, although most instructors will not allow you to submit an essay written during a prior semester for a different class, it might be possible to combine two projects from different classes into one—but only if both professors are fully aware of and approve of what you're doing.

The Web has produced its own set of temptations to students. It might not seem like cheating when all one has to do is point and click to find some ready-made phrasing, without even needing to transcribe it. Students might genuinely believe that, if they find some information or phrasing on more than one website, it must be common knowledge or public property—forgetting that the websites themselves might have plagiarized from each other or some third source. But using any idea or information that is not common knowledge without carefully and properly acknowledging that you've done so is a form of serious academic

dishonesty that—students are often surprised to learn—instructors detect easily. Instructors are familiar with the capabilities of most students and sensitive to features of individual students' writing styles. They are also familiar with the published work in their fields, well trained to recognize the contributions and stylistic habits of professional writers. A variety of specialized search engines and online services enable instructors to locate the original sources of wording and ideas stolen from published and electronic sources, often more quickly than the student was able to find it in the first place.

Plagiarism has never been so easy—but it also has never been so easy to detect. No one enjoys being suspicious, and no task is more abhorrent to an instructor than confronting a dishonest or careless student and proceeding with judicial action. It is far more satisfying to work with students to train them to use sources responsibly before questions of their integrity arise. You must do your part to make certain that you understand this material and apply it whenever you write a paper. Don't let the fear of misusing quoted material dissuade you from doing research. Instead, master the skills of quoting and paraphrasing responsibly, confident that, when you do so, you will gain a powerful and indispensable skill.

POPULAR STYLE MANUALS

Different disciplines follow different conventions for citing sources used in a project. Students might view these differences as unimportant, as if the rules are arbitrary or result from instructor preference. But formats for citing materials are not random. They have been designed by professional organizations to present citations in systematic ways that reflect the priorities and core values of that field. A book or pamphlet that presents a specific format is called a style manual. If an instructor has not specified which style manual to follow, it is a student's responsibility to ask which one to use and to follow its guidelines for formatting and printing the document and, most important, for how to arrange footnotes, endnotes, and a list of works cited. Most style manuals are available in your college or public library, and many are online. Once you have declared a major or begun graduate work within a particular field, it's a good idea to purchase a current copy of the style manual for that field. Some commonly used style manuals include the following:

- Modern Language Association's *MLA Handbook for Writers of Research Papers*, for English and modern languages
- Turabian's *Manual for Writers of Term Papers, Theses, and Dissertations*, for history and other humanities (based on the *Chicago Manual of Style*)
- *Scientific Style and Format*, published by the Council of Science Editors (CSE), for biological sciences
- *Publication Manual of the American Psychological Association* (APA) for psychology and some other social sciences
- *The ACS Style Guide*, published by the American Chemical Society (ACS), for chemistry
- *Style Manual for Political Science*, published by the American Political Science Association (APSA), for political science

This book does not present comprehensive citation formats for all fields. Because my discipline is English, my own citations will follow the format presented in the *MLA Handbook*. Whatever style manual you use for a particular course or paper, remember that the purpose of all of them is threefold:

1. To help you establish your authority and provide documentation for your claims in a systematic way

2. To help you provide your readers with all of the information they need to find your original sources and verify your claims about them

3. To provide a system for briefly identifying a source in your text with minimum textual clutter in ways that clearly refer to the fully cited work in a list at the end.

ELEMENTS REQUIRED IN A CITATION

Before you begin to gather information and take notes for a project, you need to know what sorts of information about the source you need to cite it properly—both in your list of works cited and in those portions of your text where you have used it.

If you are taking information from a book, all style sheets demand that you include in the final list:

- author
- title
- volume number (if a multivolume work)
- date of publication
- place of publication
- publisher
- page number(s)

Within your text itself, you may need to provide only the author's last name and a page number (or, for some disciplines, a year of publication). If you have used only one work by that author, it will be clear to which work in the list the name refers.

For articles, your works cited list must include:

- author
- title of the article

- title of the journal or magazine
- volume and issue numbers
- date of publication
- page number(s)

As you do with books, in your text itself you should keep your information about a source as brief as you can, providing just enough information to enable your reader to identify the full citation in your list at the end. You refer to the full citation with the author's name (if known) or with an abbreviated title of the article (if the author is not known) and the page number.

Internet sources may or may not name their authors, and they usually won't have conventional page numbers. While you still have the source before you, you might need to go to the home page or follow some other link to find out when the site was most recently revised and to find out the name of the author or sponsoring organization. If a website does not indicate a person or organization that is responsible for it, you will probably not find it to be reputable enough to be worth consulting. When this information is available, you will need to provide the name of the author or organization and the title of the site (probably abbreviated for your in-text references). In some fields, you will need to provide in your list of works cited the entire electronic address (or URL). Because an electronic source is likely to change frequently, it's also crucial that you provide the date you consulted it.

When you take notes, make sure that you distinguish carefully between quoted words and your own words, and note the page number of print sources from which the information was taken. Copy all of the necessary information (as specified above) that would allow someone else to locate that source. Spare yourself the need to return to the library simply to find the name of the publisher or the page number from which a certain quotation or paraphrased information came. *One further caution:* it is not adequate merely to list a work you have used in your works cited. You must at all times make certain that it is clear what portion of your work has used what portion of the cited source.

Following sections of this book present ways to select and incorporate material into your work that are shared by all disciplines. Get into the habit now of employing the following suggestions. You will find that all of your writing will be stronger.

WHEN DO YOU NEED TO ACKNOWLEDGE A SOURCE?

Some of what you write will come from your own observations and experience, some from class notes and discussion, some from what we call *common knowledge*, some from the assigned readings in the course, and some from works you have sought out on your own. Each of these sources merits a bit of discussion.

Obviously, you need not document in any formal way your own observations or experiences. The power of your own written voice should convince your readers of the plausibility of your own ideas and experiences.

MATERIAL FROM CLASSROOM DISCUSSION

In most circumstances, you are free to incorporate ideas that have been explored in class discussion without worrying about the ownership of those ideas. Usually you may feel free to draw on background information presented in class as you provide a context for the more focused and developed discussion in your paper. If the class lecture or discussion itself has drawn on sources, such as films or readings, then you should attribute relevant ideas to their original source. But instructors do not expect or desire credit in your paper for ideas generated in class. Two suggestions:

1. Your own paper should probably not consist entirely of ideas repeated from class. Instead, it should develop ideas more fully or apply them in new ways that demonstrate your understanding of them. Ask your instructor for suggestions if you are concerned that your paper may simply rehash ideas presented in class.
2. When you do rely on ideas or information from class, remember to explain them fully. Unless your professor specifies a particular kind of audience for your project, think of your reader as a person who is intelligent but who has not attended class. Anyone who picks up your paper should be able to understand it—not just the professor for whom you have written the paper.

COMMON KNOWLEDGE

The category of information we call *common knowledge* is a more complex matter. Common knowledge includes broad historical facts that are not the conclusions or discoveries of a particular author, for example the fact that John Kennedy was the 35th President of the United States, or that Emily Brontë died the year after *Wuthering Heights* was published, or that under normal atmospheric pressure, water boils at 100 degrees Celsius. Even if you have to look up common-knowledge facts like these in a reference work, you do not need to cite your source. Nor do you have to document commonly known generalizations, such as the assumption that the Romantic Era in British literature was a time of intense literary innovation, or that computers have revolutionized communication, or that laboratory experimentation with animals is controversial. When you are beginning your studies of a particular subject, you might not always be able to tell easily what is common knowledge within a discipline and what isn't. But as you read more widely in a field with an eye toward what the other authors assume is shared information, you will be better able to assess what information properly belongs to particular authors. Two cautions:

1. Even if you judge a bit of information to be shared publicly, be careful not to represent another writer's phrasing of this common knowledge as your own. Although the information may be common knowledge, a specific writer's expression of the information is still the property of that writer.
2. If you cannot decide if some information needs to be credited to an author, provide a reference giving such credit. When in doubt, cite your source.

Common knowledge also includes traditional tales, folk literature, and folk wisdom—tales or observations that are handed down without the knowledge of who wrote the tale or made the observation. Many fairy tales—for instance those of Mother Goose—or age-old songs and jokes—such as "Three Blind Mice" and "Why did the chicken cross the road?"—do not require documentation of the source. Nor would you need to provide a note crediting some source with the observation that a dog is a man's best friend, that absence makes the heart grow fonder, or that a bird in the hand is worth two in the bush. Many clichés or sayings fall into this category, though where authors are known, you should mention them. You should, for example, acknowledge that it was Alexander Pope who wrote "To err is human, to forgive divine," or Thomas Paine who wrote "These are the times that try men's souls." But generalized, common-sense observations do not usually need to be credited to a source. Be forewarned, however, that most readers will not continue read-ing something that tells them things they already know, and they will probably be irritated if your phrasing is hackneyed or your observations trite. If you use clichés in formal writing, use them in some fresh or unexpected way, or your readers will probably assume that you have nothing new to say and may lose interest in what you've written.

USING TEXTBOOKS AS SOURCES

When you draw on information from a course textbook or from a source you have found on your own, you need to credit the source for all information drawn from it that is not common knowledge. For informal papers in which you refer only to class textbooks, professors may not demand that you give a complete reference that includes all of the publication facts. Ask your professor if it is acceptable merely to specify the author and title and put the page number from which the information was taken in parentheses at the end of the sentence. Even if the source is a class textbook and the author and title are clear from the context (the assignment is a paper on *Wuthering Heights*, for example), you must at least cite the edition and page number because your professor will want to be able to locate the exact page from which you are getting the information, whether you quote it directly or paraphrase it. Even when you are writing a short homework or in-class assignment, you should acknowledge material that is not your own. You should provide proper citations of your sources not merely to avoid plagiarism, but to empower your writing with authority, evidence, and illustrative detail.

Remember to acknowledge the source of any visual material you have included in your essay, unless that material is truly in public domain or is provided by your word processing program as clip art. For example, if you incorporate photographs or drawings in your written project (and you did not create them), you must acknowledge the source of this material. A brief reference in a caption for the picture, followed by a full citation in your list of works cited, will usually suffice for class assignments.

USING SOURCES IN CLASS PRESENTATIONS

In the give and take of ordinary class discussion, no one expects or desires attention to source material beyond mentioning an author's name or, at most, a page number of a book if others have copies of it with them. But a report to the class is a different matter. The more formal, lengthy, and public the presentation, the more thoroughly you should acknowledge the sources you have used.

If your report is entirely verbal (without use of PowerPoint or other visual material), acknowledge your use of information that is not common knowledge by referring to the name of the author of a publication as you present the information from that source. At the end of your talk, you can offer to share a printed list of the works you cite, a list that you should put in the proper format for the discipline. Such a practice doesn't add to the length of your talk, nor does it add any tedium or clutter. It demonstrates your care about ownership of ideas, and it adds to the authority of your comments by noting the studies you have consulted. Offering to share the citations list shows your respect not only for the published authors but for the other students in the course, as well.

If you are augmenting your presentation with PowerPoint, the visual text gives you a ready place to acknowledge source material. The PowerPoint text should not exactly duplicate what you are saying, or the effect will be redundant and tedious to your audience. You might signal the architecture of your talk with an outline, but you should resist the impulse to project your text as you speak it. In general, reserve the images that you include for things that are best presented visually. You might want to display an important quotation that you're planning to discuss, and such a passage should include a citation of its source. You might use a diagram that illustrates relationships among the things you are discussing. If you use a diagram that you have found in print or on the Web, be certain to provide a full citation for it.

Whenever you include graphic materials, be very careful to assess the degree to which they are protected by copyright laws. Of course, you may use clip art as freely as you might any of the graphics enhancements that come with the software you're using. But if you include a photograph or a film or audio clip, you must acknowledge the proper source for the material. That source is probably not the search engine you employed to find it. For example, if you wanted an image of nineteenth-century garment industry workers, you could conduct an image search on Google to find a wide assortment of images. If you choose one to use, the proper source to cite would not be Google—cite the website to which Google directed you. You should go to that site to find the name of the author or sponsoring organization, the title of the site, the URL, and so forth. The same would be true for film clips or sound recordings that you are incorporating into your presentation. Make certain to find all of the information required for a full citation of the actual source, and include that citation (probably in a modestly sized font) on the screen during your presentation. Showing such care is important in establishing the authenticity of the materials you're including and in avoiding improper or unethical uses of published material. If you are using images, photos, and clips to complete a class project, make sure you acknowledge the proper source in proper form. In these circumstances, with this limited purpose and with proper citation, the law generally grants you this fair use of the material.

If your presentation is going to be posted on a course webpage or in any other way made available on the Internet, your use of such materials without proper citation could involve more than academic dishonesty. It could involve legal matters of violated copyright. Using such copyrighted material for purposes other than completion of an assignment for a class might require you to pay permissions fees and use specific language in your acknowledgments. Public and for-profit use of copyrighted tables, charts, poems, songs, film clips, sound recordings, and photographs nearly always requires written permission from the owner of the material.

WHEN SHOULD YOU PARAPHRASE AND WHEN SHOULD YOU QUOTE?

Done properly, paraphrasing information gives you remarkable flexibility and, by permitting you to select only the information most relevant to your topic, it enables you to express your ideas with a minimum of verbiage. In short, it ensures that all of the information is pertinent, and it helps you to write with economy and vigor. When readers encounter information paraphrased or summarized from one of your sources, they do not have to move between writing by you and that by another author, shifting to a new voice, a new style, a different pace and context. When you paraphrase well, you do your reader a great service, because you've selected, organized, and phrased the information to suit your purposes, all in a manner that preserves a continuity of style and emphasis. But paraphrasing requires more work of you than simply copying someone else's words.

It is appropriate for you to paraphrase, instead of quoting, whenever the wording itself is less important to the purpose of your writing than the information it presents. If all you need from an economic study, for example, is the distressing information that, nationally, a woman with a college degree has the same earning potential as a male high school dropout, simply paraphrase the conclusions of the study in your own words and state your source, rather than quoting the study. Citing a statistic, a relatively unknown fact, a bit of information embedded in a study that otherwise is not relevant to your topic—in all of these situations, it is advisable to paraphrase rather than to quote. Conversely, if the source itself is important to your topic, if the original wording helps you to illustrate your point, if the opinion expressed in the passage is controversial or highly unusual, or if the work itself *is* your subject (as in a paper on a literary work or an analysis of a text), then it is advisable to quote the actual words the original author used.

The next time you watch a televised news program, notice how the news writers and reporters use sources to establish the credibility of their reporting. The orchestrated movements to and from different locations, to and from other correspondents, other cameras and voices—these movements are analogous to an author's presentation of information in nonfiction writing. If they chose to, news anchors could present all of the news stories in their (or their news editor's) own words. Actually, doing so would provide better quality of both visual images and recorded language than the grainy, sometimes poorly focused film footage that is shot by foreign correspondents with their handheld cameras in the heat of battle. Many news anchors do present much of the information themselves, particularly economic news (which doesn't film very dramatically) or stories for which they have no taped footage. But roughly half of the time, they turn the story over to a person in the field, to an eyewitness speaking without revising, or to a correspondent who narrates over some film footage, blurred by the processes of photography, distanced by the satellite transmission. Why? The answer is probably obvious. Going to the sources that are close to the story, to the people who are more authoritative than are the anchors themselves, contributes to their credibility. The news anchors become more authoritative for knowing when to let someone else be the authority. They introduce the news item and the taped footage, they let us know who is speaking, then they show us a tape, frequently following the segment with some kind of concluding remarks to give the story a sense of closure. Any broadcast of a news program will demonstrate a similar use of primary source material. Even though the conventions of video documentation differ from those of printed writing—for example, there are no footnotes in a newscast—the purpose of such material is evident.

Paraphrase (with proper citations) when all you need is the information itself.

Quote when your source is important, when you can gain authority by turning to another author.

HOW SHOULD YOU PARAPHRASE INFORMATION FROM A SOURCE?

Once you've decided that the occasion calls for paraphrasing, you need to do several things.

SELECTING INFORMATION FROM YOUR SOURCE

First, you need to select the information relevant to your topic and make certain that you completely rephrase the ideas—in your own words. Do not use any phrases, syntax, or organization that appeared in the original work. These are the author's personal property, and representing segments or features of a passage as your own constitutes plagiarism.

An Example of Paraphrasing

Suppose you are writing a paper on blue jeans as a cultural phenomenon, exploring what the enduring popularity of blue jeans illustrates about our culture. You find an essay in *American Heritage*, "The Jeaning of America—and the World," by Carin

Quinn, in which she writes the following about Levi's jeans (on page 18):

> The pants have become a tradition, and along the way have acquired a history of their own—so much so that the company has opened a museum in San Francisco. There was, for example, the turn-of-the-century trainman who replaced a faulty coupling with a pair of jeans; the Wyoming man who used his jeans as a towrope to haul his car out of a ditch; the Californian who found several pairs in an abandoned mine, wore them, then discovered they were sixty-three years old and still as good as new and turned them over to the Smithsonian as a tribute to their toughness. And then there is the particularly terrifying story of the careless construction worker who dangled fifty-two stories above the street until rescued, his sole support the Levi's belt loop through which his rope was hooked.

You decide that the information about the museum and her examples of heroically strong jeans would strengthen your argument about what the jeans symbolize, and you write the following:

> The jeans have earned a history all their own—to such an extent that the Levi's corporation even operates a museum of jeans in San Francisco. The museum presents the stories of the trainman who hitched two trains together with a pair of jeans, of the Wyoming man who towed his car out of a ditch using a pair of jeans, of the Californian who found several pairs in an abandoned mine, put them on, discovered they were still good as new after sixty-three years, and donated them to the Smithsonian as a tribute to their toughness. One especially horrifying story is that of the construction worker who lost his footing and dangled some fifty stories over the street, hanging

only from the Levi's belt loop which his rope was hooked on. [improper paraphrase—plagiarism]

If you left this paragraph in your paper—even if you provided a note naming Carin Quinn as your source, and even if you didn't intend to deceive anyone—you would be guilty of plagiarism. Even though much of the paragraph has been rephrased, much of it hasn't been. This paragraph is organized exactly like the original, and much of the rewriting is merely substitution of synonyms for her original words, relying far too heavily on her syntax. The phrase "particularly terrifying," for example, is replaced by "especially horrifying," with much of the original sentence left intact. The exact repetition of "found several pairs in an abandoned mine" and of the phrase "tribute to their toughness" is especially damning. If this wording is important enough to repeat verbatim, then you should quote it; otherwise, the passage should be completely reworded.

A far better example of paraphrasing, one that incorporates Quinn's ideas into the author's own argument, would be the following use of the material:

Every morning, as you slip into your jeans, you put on a part of American history. You might merely be seeking warmth on a cold day or trying to make yourself decent for a walk downtown, but your jeans bring with them a long cultural tradition and probably more legendary strength than you'll ever need to run your errands. According to Carin Quinn, a pair of the original Levi's served once as a rope for a man in Wyoming who needed to tow his car out of a ditch. A trainman once used a pair of the jeans to couple together two railway cars when the original coupling had broken. And when a hapless construction worker lost his footing fifty-two stories above the earth, one loop of his jeans was sufficient to hold him until help arrived (18). The Levi's corporation is well aware of its image. The leather patch with the Levi trademark shows a pair of jeans pulled between two horses. Most days you probably won't be repairing trains, dangling overhead, or deliberately frustrating the movement of horses, but wearing blue jeans symbolically connects you with the strength, ingenuity, preparedness, and even heroism embodied in these legends about the jeans.

Granted, this paragraph contains many ideas not found in the original source. And Quinn's paragraph presents information not included in this passage. But that's part of the point. You shouldn't simply repeat ideas you've found elsewhere; you should incorporate those ideas into a context all your own. And you should make clear which of the ideas in the paragraph derive from Quinn's work and which are entirely your own. Including the author's name at the beginning and a page or note number (depending on your style sheet) at the end of the paraphrased material makes it clear which information came from the source and which didn't. When you do find some useful information in a source you've consulted, you should explicitly name the author, select only those details that suit your purpose, phrase them in wording that is entirely your own, provide the page number, and then print the full publishing information in a list of works cited at the end of your paper.

GIVING CREDIT TO YOUR SOURCE

The second thing you must do has already been mentioned but bears repeating here: Even if you are not quoting actual words, you need to give credit for the information, and you need to make clear exactly what has come from your source. Sometimes students believe that all they need to do if they've drawn information from a source is provide the author's name in parentheses (or a note number) at the end of the paragraph containing the paraphrased material, confident that they've given credit where credit is due. This practice, however, is dangerously ambiguous and even misleading. A citation at the end of a paragraph implies that *all* of the material in the paragraph had its origin in the cited source, even if the paragraph is a mix of borrowed information and original insight. This practice might attribute ideas to the cited author that he or she did not develop, and it completely muddies the distinction between your own ideas and those of the other author. For example, in the last sample paragraph on jeans, if I had not mentioned the author's name where I did and if I had waited until the end of the paragraph to provide the page (or note) number, I would have inaccurately represented all of the ideas in the paragraph as Quinn's, thereby denying myself credit for the ideas that precede and follow the paraphrased material. Quinn does not make the observation that Levi's represents American ingenuity and preparedness for adversity. That idea is mine, and I shouldn't allow mere sloppiness with writing technique to rob me of credit for the discovery. Nor should I claim that Quinn advances ideas that she doesn't. Misrepresenting a source in such a way is also dishonest.

The author's name at the beginning of the paraphrased material and the page number at the end of it function a bit as the beginning and ending quotation marks would if the material were quoted—they set off the cited information from your own, signaling its different status from the other words, identifying the source with maximum clarity and minimal distraction. In short, think of embedding the paraphrased material in your own prose as a kind of linguistic bracketing or fencing off of the information in as clear a way as possible, so as not to give the author too little credit—or too much.

THE IMPORTANCE OF ACCURACY IN PARAPHRASING

Finally, you need to make certain that your synopsis of the author's ideas accurately reflects the author's actual statement. It probably goes without saying that you shouldn't misrepresent a paraphrased source, yet often students seem rather cavalier about restating others' ideas. Notice how frequently letters to the editor in your newspaper attempt to correct a perceived misreading or misrepresentation of an earlier letter. In the heat of the debate about social or political issues, people often say things imprecisely and misread the letters of others. Most of your sources are far more carefully composed than such letters. So should be your reading of them. Imagine that the authors whose words you are paraphrasing are going to read your synopsis of what

"That's the last time he'll disseminate disparaging remarks and slanderous disinformation through out-of-context misquoting in this town."

© Tom Cheney / The New Yorker Collection / www.cartoonbank.com

they said. Will they feel that their views have been accurately and fairly represented? You may certainly disagree with what an author says in print, but it only helps to establish your credibility if you present those ideas fairly (maybe even quoting especially pertinent lines), before going on to demonstrate what is wrong with the author's position.

The focus and length of your project should guide you as you decide how much of the source you plan to use. It is usually best not to use only a general or concluding remark as if it is sufficient by itself to constitute evidence or argument. Neglecting to explain the author's reasons for her or his position and simply using a general phrase from the work will make it seem as if you are content to rely on authority assertions rather than to critically assess the ideas. Whether you agree with or challenge the published view (paraphrased or quoted), it helps you to establish your thoroughness and fairness if you attend to the reasoning behind an author's conclusions as you use the material.

HOW SHOULD YOU QUOTE MATERIAL FROM A SOURCE?

HOW MUCH TO QUOTE

Students sometimes wonder what proportion of their papers should be quoted material and what should be original words of their own. At one extreme, their papers might consist of lengthy quoted passages, stitched together with a few transitions of their own, as if writing is like assembling a patchwork quilt out of fragments of others' cloth. At the other extreme, students might quote only once, leaving most of their paragraphs without quotations to serve as illustration or evidence. Either extreme is disproportionate. Think of quoting as a valuable means of developing and supporting ideas—not as the means of presenting the ideas themselves. In some cases, quotations will be the best form your evidence could take, and neglecting to include relevant quotations could mean neglecting to provide convincing illustrative material. When you are revising your paper, read through it once without reading the quoted words. If your paper makes little sense without the quotations, you've probably attempted to make them do too much. Your words should present your argument; the quotations are only supportive material—valuable and essential to convincing your reader but never the primary means of presenting information.

HOW TO PRESENT A QUOTATION

Once you've decided that it is appropriate to quote, you need to decide how much of the passage merits being presented in your paper. It may be that the information you need is entangled in a long sentence or paragraph, most of which is beside your immediate point. In this case, were you to quote the entire sentence or paragraph, you would needlessly divert your reader's attention from your immediate topic. You can quote passages of virtually any length: a word, a phrase, a sentence, even a paragraph. But whatever you quote should be entirely relevant to your purpose, and the longer the passage you quote, the greater should be your attention to the material. Most of the time it would be rhetorically ineffective to quote a long passage, unless you plan to analyze or interpret it at some length, following the quotation. In most instances, your task will be to select a phrase or sentence that best illustrates the point you are making, and, taking great care to copy the material exactly as it is written, fit the quoted author's words into your own, making certain that you mark the quoted passage with quotation marks, name the source of the material (if it isn't already clear in the paragraph), and work the phrases into your own in a way that produces grammatical and coherent statements. If you fit a quoted phrase into a sentence, check for two things:

1. Between the opening and closing quotation marks, every symbol should be reproduced exactly at it appears in the original, unless you've clearly indicated what changes you made in the ways explained below.

2. Try reading your paragraph as if there were no quotation marks present. All of the words, quoted and unquoted, must function together in grammatical and coherent ways.

Never present a quotation as a completely separate sentence. Always introduce it in some way. The quotation marks by themselves are not adequate to explain the differences between your voice and that of the person you are quoting, who probably is exploring a topic different from yours, in a different style, in a different verb tense, and with a different point of view or choice of pronouns. Given the potential for confusion and incoherence as you switch from your voice to another's and back again, you should take some special care to ease your readers' way to and from the quoted material. Further, the presence of quotation marks (without any introduction or transition) is not a sufficient signal that the material has come from a source, because writers use quotation marks for some purposes other than quoting. They might mark a word that they are using in a special way or mark a word that they are discussing. Some authors who choose to use a slang expression will surround the expression with quotation marks as if to apologize for using the phrase. It is not a particularly admirable practice, but it is a fairly common one. Don't "fly off the handle" at such practices; instead, keep your "cool." The important point here is to introduce all quotations in ways that indicate you are quoting, that identify the source, and that suggest the significance of what the person is saying.

As you lead into a quoted passage, you should consider what sorts of information about your source the reader needs to know to understand the significance of the quotation.

- Does the author have a position or credentials that are relevant to the quoted statement?

- Is the date of the statement important enough to note as you introduce it?
- Was the quoted passage published originally as a part of a major study?
- Has the author employed a particular research methodology that might contextualize the study within the field?
- Has the author made use of important or unusual materials?
- Is the journal or other medium in which the piece appears particularly noteworthy?

If you know this kind of information and it helps to establish the context of the material within the field of your topic, you should consider including it as you introduce a quoted passage. Think of the reasons that you consulted the source in the first place and the reasons why you selected the passage that you did.

If you can signal these reasons to your reader as you introduce the material, your reader might better understand the relationship of the quoted passage to your essay. At the very least, you should convey that the quoted material comes from a source:

"According to one study . . ."
"One author puts it this way . . ."
"A later report claims that . . ."

Better yet, name the source:

"Miller argues that . . ."
"Johnston, who studied the mosquito for fifteen years, postulates that . . ."
"The chief engineer on the project, Eliza Swaney, observes . . ."

And if the passage is important, alert your reader to the nature of its significance or to its context in your work:

"Jonathan Alder offers a contrasting view . . ."
"Linkholder's rebuttal shows her dependence on Connelly's theorem . . ."
"Note the veiled anger in Cramer's reply."

Your objective is to signal your movements to and from a quotation with maximum clarity, continuity, and context, and to encourage your reader to predict what will follow in a quotation. As you read authors you admire in the field for which you are writing, get in the habit of noticing how the authors have chosen to do what they do. When you encounter writing done well, read it carefully, not just for the information you need, but to learn from the example alternate ways of meeting your needs as a writer.

HOW TO SHOW ADDITIONS AND DELETIONS IN A QUOTATION

Between the opening set of quotation marks and the closing pair, every word, letter, and punctuation mark must be exactly as it appears in the original. You can change some of the things in a quotation—adding or deleting words—but only if you indicate that you have done so and only if your change does not distort the meaning of what you've quoted. One change is permitted—actually required—within a quotation: if the source itself quotes something else, you change the double quotation marks to single ones, so that they are not confused with the ones that you have provided. You should also change the final punctuation mark in your quotation of a passage to suit your own grammatical needs (see below), in effect stopping your quoting before the final symbol. But if grammar demands that you add a word, change the tense of a quoted verb, or clarify the reference of a quoted pronoun, for instance, you should do so by enclosing your change in square brackets (not parentheses).

If for reasons of clarity, grammar, or brevity, you decide to delete a word or phrase from within a series of quoted words, put in its place an ellipsis, three spaced dots . . ., to show your reader that you've left something out. If you are quoting a passage that itself already makes use of an ellipsis, place the periods you add within square brackets to distinguish between those you added to show your deletion and those already in the text you quote. In this situation, you should space once before the opening bracket, *between* the periods themselves, and once after the closing bracket, so that your ellipsis looks like this: [. . .]. If the passage you are quoting does not already make use of an ellipsis, simply add the required periods without the brackets. If quoting the passage requires extensive bracketing and ellipses, to the extent that you must undergo all sorts of grammatical or typographic contortions, consider paraphrasing the material or quoting only the most relevant phrases or words. The following examples will illustrate how to use square brackets and the ellipsis.

Assume for the moment that you are writing an essay on Fitzgerald's *The Great Gatsby*, exploring the ways in which the narrator, Nick Carraway, is biased as he relates the events. Because your topic is a work of literature, and especially because you are attempting to show how the narrator's language reveals his attitudes, you will frequently wish to quote from the novel. You will find no more direct source of evidence to convince skeptical readers than quoting the actual novel.

Using Square Brackets to Mark Words Added to a Quotation

Original (from page 39 of Fitzgerald's *The Great Gatsby*):
In his blue gardens men and girls came and went like moths among the whisperings and the champagne and the stars.

Your use of the passage (the page number follows the passage): Nick Carraway, the narrator in the novel, says that "In his [Gatsby's] blue gardens men and girls came and went like moths among the whisperings and the champagne and the stars" (39).

Explanation:

By itself, the original "his" in the passage would have incorrectly implied that the gardens under discussion were Nick's instead of Gatsby's. In this case, a more graceful way of clarifying the meaning of the pronoun would be to provide a referent for "his" as you introduce the quotation, as in the following:

> Early in the novel, Nick reveals his contempt for Gatsby's guests: "In his blue gardens men and girls came and went like moths among the whisperings and the champagne and the stars" (39).

This use of the material avoids the clutter of the brackets and better alerts the reader to notice Nick's judgment of the guests. Yet another way to use this material (and other relevant details from the novel) might be to write the following:

> Despite Nick's early claim that he is "inclined to reserve all judgments" (1), he says that Tom has "a cruel body" (7), and he refers to Gatsby's guests as "moths" (39).

This might be an even better use of the material, depending on the focus and context of the essay. It explains why it matters that Nick is in fact judgmental, and it makes use of selected phrases or words that illustrate this trait. Within the pairs of quotation marks, every word is identical to the original. And each quotation is followed by the number of the page on which the passage appears. If you can rework your use of a passage to avoid using the brackets, do so. But if you need to change something, employ the brackets to signify that change. Following is one more example of how bracketed information may clarify the meaning of a pronoun. While it is clear in the novel that Nick is speaking of Gatsby in these lines, removing the passage from its context requires that you clarify the meaning in your context.

Original (from page 102):
For several weeks I didn't see him or hear his voice on the phone—mostly I was in New York, trotting around with Jordan and trying to ingratiate myself with her senile aunt—but finally I went over to his house one Sunday afternoon.

Your use of the material:
Nick makes it clear that the only events of that summer that interest him now are those involving Gatsby. At one point he alludes to other events, but he quickly returns to his real subject:

> For several weeks I didn't see [Gatsby] or hear his voice on the phone—mostly I was in New York, trotting around with Jordan and trying to ingratiate myself with her senile aunt—but finally I went over to his house one Sunday afternoon. (102)

Here Nick summarizes "several weeks" in only nineteen words, those weeks not mattering because they didn't involve his hero, Gatsby.

Explanation:

Notice again the simple way you can clear up a potentially confusing pronoun with information enclosed in brackets. Notice also that, when the quoted passage is relatively long (more than three typed lines), you present it in "block" format: you set it off from the rest of your text by indenting it. When you present block quotations, you should not enclose the material in quotation marks unless they appear in the original. Setting it off in block format already tells the reader that the material is quoted. The page number or any other parenthetical publication information follows the period in a block quotation. Notice also that the paragraph does not end simply because I presented a block quotation. I followed the passage with attention to its details, connecting it to the idea I'm developing. Beginning and closing lines in paragraphs are positions of extreme emphasis; don't leave your reader dangling at the end of block quotations. Resume your analysis, closing the paragraph by returning to your immediate point.

If your paper is written in the present tense and you wish to quote something written in the past tense, bracket the part of the verb you change:

Original (from p. 80):
He had waited five years and bought a mansion where he dispensed starlight to casual moths—so that he could "come over" some afternoon to a stranger's garden.

Your use of the material:
Nick implies throughout the novel that Gatsby's guests are undeserving of his social efforts, saying that Gatsby "dispense[s] starlight to casual moths" (80).

Notice, as always, the quoted material is introduced in some way that makes its source and its importance clear to your reader.

Using the Ellipsis to Indicate That You Deleted Words from a Quotation

If you decide, in the interests of brevity and relevance, to leave out some material from within a quoted passage, provide the ellipsis (three spaced periods) to show it. The deletion, obviously, should not change the meaning of the passage, nor should it produce a series of words that do not fit grammatically with the rest of your writing. If you are omitting an entire sentence or more from within a quotation, you should provide the regular period at the end of the sentence before the deleted material, and then provide the usual ellipsis (three spaced periods) to show that one or more sentences have been deleted. Do not begin or end a quotation with ellipses, especially if you are quoting only a word or a phrase. Surrounding the quoted material with ellipses only adds unnecessary clutter. If the passage itself already contains an ellipsis, place the ellipsis within square brackets. The brackets will enable your reader to distinguish between the ellipsis you have added and the spaced periods used for some other purpose by the author of the original passage.

Suppose you are writing an essay on the psychology behind the marketing of sport utility vehicles. You find an essay by Malcolm Gladwell called "Big and Bad: How the S.U.V. Ran Over Automotive Safety" (*New Yorker*, 12 January 2004). Because Gladwell incorporates in his essay various studies and interviews with automotive marketing specialists, you decide to use some of the material from the following passage:

Original (from p. 31):
The S.U.V. boom represents, then, a shift in how we conceive of safety—from active to passive. It's what happens when a larger number of drivers conclude, consciously or otherwise, that the extra thirty feet that the TrailBlazer takes to come to a stop doesn't really matter, that the tractor-trailer will hit them anyway, and that they are better off treating accidents as inevitable rather than avoidable. "The metric that people use is size," says Stephen Popiel, a vice-president of Millward Brown Goldfarb, in Toronto, one of the leading automotive market-

research firms. "The bigger something is, the safer it is. In the consumer's mind, the basic equation is, If I were to take this vehicle and drive it into this brick wall, the more metal there is in front of me the better off I'll be."

Your use of the material:
One of the reasons that S.U.V.s are so profitable to manufacture is that, classified as trucks, they need not meet government safety standards established for passenger cars. Yet nearly all of the advertisements for S.U.V.s promote safety as the vehicles' chief advantage. Seated far from the road, surrounded by massive expanses of cushioned plastic and many of the amenities of home, drivers of S.U.V.s certainly *feel* safe, despite the loss of maneuverability and braking power as the size and weight of vehicles increase. "The S.U.V. boom," according to Malcolm Gladwell, "represents . . . a shift in how [American drivers] conceive of safety—from active to passive." A passive view of safety reflects a general assumption that people don't have much control over what happens to them, so they should be prepared for the worst and treat "accidents as inevitable rather than avoidable." Gladwell quotes market-researcher Stephen Popiel: "The metric that people use is size. . . . The bigger something is, the safer it is" (31). As people feel safer and less responsible for what happens, they do things they'd do if they *weren't* driving—talking on the phone, watching videos, reaching for the nearby cup-holder. As Gladwell notes, "That feeling of safety isn't the solution; it's the problem" (32).

Explanation:

This passage illustrates a number of things. In the first quoted line, an ellipsis replaces the word *then*, a transition in Gladwell's essay that doesn't function well in the new context. The deleted word is within a single quoted sentence, so there's no added pe-riod—only the three required for an ellipsis. This ellipsis is not placed in square brackets because Gladwell's original passage contains no ellipsis of his own. Replacing Gladwell's "we" with the bracketed "American drivers" keeps the point of view con-sistent with the third person used in the rest of the paragraph. The brackets acknowledge the change. Because the same page of Gladwell's essay is used again twice in the same paragraph, the page number is not presented until the final use of the material. It will be clear that the quotations are from the same page. Note that the page number is not part of the quotation but it is part of the sentence, so it is placed after the quotation marks but be-fore the period. In general, select what is relevant and important enough to quote; use the ellipsis to indicate that you have left out material within the original; place the ellipsis within square brackets only if the original passage itself uses spaced periods; use square brackets to designate material added to the original; intro-duce quoted sources explicitly in your text; make certain that all words (quoted and unquoted) fit together in grammatically com-plete ways; and provide page numbers (of print sources) after the quotation marks but before the final punctuation of the sentence.

WRITING ABOUT LITERATURE

When you are writing an analytical essay about a work of litera-ture, much of your purpose is to show your reader *how* the work means what it does—not just to state what it means about a par-ticular topic. To help convey your familiarity with the work, keep your focus on the text you are discussing, quoting frequently to establish your authority in discussing the text and to keep your attention and your readers' focused on the work. Learn to vary the kinds of references you make to the work. Occasionally, an entire sentence merits quoting. More rarely, a longer passage. You should also learn to interweave significant quoted phrases from the work into your own sentences. These brief noun phrases or verbs or adjectives help to convey the tone and flavor of the work you are discussing, and they reassure your reader that your claims have a basis in the text itself. As you select such phrases and integrate them into your sentences, remember that all words (quoted and unquoted) must fit together grammatically as if there were no quotation marks: verbs require subjects that make sense, and pronouns need clear referents, and so forth, whether they are yours or the original author's. The following three examples, from an essay about William Blake's "The Chimney Sweeper" from his *Songs of Innocence*, illustrate a variety of kinds of uses of brief quoted phrases:

> In the *Innocence* version of "The Chimney Sweeper," the Angel in Tom's dream, who "open'd the coffins & set them all free," does so with a "bright key," suggestive of both the light visible at the top of a chimney and, worse, the possible fire at the bottom (lines 14, 13).

> The unnamed older sweeper in the poem does not complain or whine when he reports in his stoic, matter-of-fact way, "my father sold me" (2).

> The hope in Tom's dream would be particularly powerful to an orphaned sweeper: the dream of being able to "wash in the river"; to run "down a green plain, leaping, laughing"; and, above all, to have a father, a divine one at that (16, 15).

Notice that the citations for the quoted phrases do not include the page number from the anthology, because the numbers would all be the same. It's a brief poem, all on one page. If the text you are quoting is a poem, provide line numbers for the passages you quote, providing the word *line* or *lines* in your first citation to establish your practice in the essay and then providing only the numbers in subsequent citations. If you are quoting a verse play or a long poem, your instructor might prefer that you cite the division (act, scene, part, canto) and line with a period dividing the two numbers.

As you are fitting quotations into your own writing, it's good to remember to keep your own subjects and verbs close together so your sentences remain clear and easy to read. Resist the temptation to put a lengthy quotation (itself, perhaps, a complete sentence) in the middle of one of your sentences. Relocate such passages to the end.

Ineffective example:
The persona's reassurance to little Tom, "when your head's bare, / You know that the soot cannot spoil your white hair," might comfort Tom, but it's every bit as horrible as the precept with which the poem ends (7–8).

Revised example:
The persona reassures little Tom with a comfort as horrible as the precept at the poem's end: "Hush Tom! Never mind it, for when your head's bare, / You know that the soot cannot spoil your white hair" (7–8).

With the proper symbols, you can add, replace, or delete words within quoted material and enjoy considerable flexibility in the way you use quotations. In general, try to keep your use of quotations as straightforward and uncomplicated as you can. Your reader should always be able to tell what has been taken verbatim from a source and what you have done to change the material. Next are a few more suggestions for punctuating quotations within your work.

HOW SHOULD
YOU PUNCTUATE
QUOTATIONS?

INTRODUCING A QUOTATION

If you are introducing a quotation with a grammatically complete statement (an independent clause), follow the opening with a colon:

> According to Naomi Klein, the increase in the power of corporations can be traced back to a single, seemingly harmless idea that was popular in the mid-1980s: "that successful corporations must primarily produce brands, as opposed to products" (3).

In this example, the part of the sentence that precedes the colon is grammatically complete. It could end where the colon is without resulting in a sentence fragment. A colon is the proper punctuation mark only if what precedes the colon is grammatically complete. What follows the colon may be a word, a phrase, a sentence, or even a paragraph.

Use a comma if what you are quoting is a complete sentence but your introduction to it makes the quotation itself the necessary object of a verb:

He said, "I never met her before that occasion."

In this sentence, the verb *said* requires an object (in this case the quotation itself). "He said" is grammatically incomplete, so it is followed by a comma, not a colon. Rephrased as a complete sentence, the introductory clause requires a colon:

His denial was emphatic: "I never met her before that occasion."

In the above sentence, if a comma followed the word *emphatic*, the result would be a comma splice, because two grammatically independent clauses would be joined without a conjunction.

When you quote single words or phrases from an author, your punctuation should be exactly the same as if the quotation marks were not there. Don't insert unnecessary commas. As I did above, when I wrote that Nick called Gatsby's guests "moths," you should simply use the quoted word without any preceding comma.

ENDING A QUOTATION

At the end of a quoted passage, you should provide whatever end punctuation serves your grammatical needs. If you stop quoting from a passage that ends with a punctuation mark, you may drop the original punctuation mark and provide whatever is grammatically appropriate within your text. In American usage, commas and periods are always placed *inside* the final set of quotation marks, unless you provide a page number in parentheses after the quotation. Note the difference in the two following examples:

> Throughout *America's Meltdown*, John Arden calls American culture the lowest common denominator or "LCD society."

> John Arden calls American culture the lowest common denominator or "LCD society" (1).

The page number in parentheses is not part of the quotation, so it is placed outside the quotation marks, but it is part of the sentence, so it precedes the final period. When a sentence ends with a quotation followed by a parenthetical citation, do not add a comma before the citation. Semicolons, colons, question marks, and exclamation points always appear *outside* the final quotation marks (unless the question mark or exclamation is part of the quotation).

PRESENTING QUOTATIONS WITHIN QUOTATIONS

When you quote a passage that itself uses quotation marks, change the author's original double quotation marks to single ones to indicate a quotation within a quotation:

> **Original** (from page 7 of Rachel Carson's *The Silent Spring*):
> Since the mid-1940s over 200 basic chemicals have been created for use in killing insects, weeds, rodents, and other organisms described in the modern vernacular as "pests"; and they are sold under several thousand different brand names.

> **Your use of the material:**
> According to Rachel Carson, more than 200 chemicals are used to kill "organisms described in the modern vernacular as 'pests'" (7).

Notice that the original double quotation marks are changed to single ones to distinguish them from the ones you've provided. Because the quoted passage is presented in the text, instead of set off in block format, the page number is placed outside the quotation marks but before the period. If no page number were provided, the final period would be placed inside *both* sets of closing quotation marks.

PUNCTUATING TITLES

Whenever you provide the title of a work, you should punctuate it properly. Titles of long works, originally published independently, should be underlined (or italicized). Titles of novels, magazines, plays, books, television shows, films, and speeches are all underlined. Titles of essays, short poems, short songs, articles, episodes from a television series, and short stories are all placed in quotation marks. If you quote a published review that punctuates titles differently, you may change the way the title is presented in what you quote without indicating that you have done so. Even in a title in your list of works cited, if you are listing a work with a title within its title, change the capitalization and punctuation to match the formatting required in your field. Most magazines, for example, put titles of films and of books in quotation marks. If you quote such a review, you should underline the title or italicize it to attain stylistic consistency in what you've written. Do not use both italics and underlining in the same document (because underlining signals to a designer that the title should be in italics). Use whichever symbol (italics or underlining) is recommended in the field in which you are writing or whichever is required by your instructor.

QUOTING POETRY

One final situation needs explanation here: quoting lines of poetry. One important difference between poetry and prose is that lines of poetry are usually shorter than the full printed width of the paper. The line breaks are an important feature of the poem's form. Thus, if you are quoting a section of a poem that, in the original, runs onto another line, you should indicate where the line ends by providing a spaced slash mark where the break occurs. For example, the opening sentence in Adrienne Rich's "Diving into the Wreck" reads (lines 1–7),

> First having read the book of myths,
> and loaded the camera,
> and checked the edge of the knife-blade,
> I put on
> the body-armor of black rubber
> the absurd flippers
> the grave and awkward mask.

If you wish to quote the entire sentence, present it in block format, as I did above, preserving all of the original spacing and line breaks (without slash marks). If you wish to quote fewer than three lines, present them as part of your regular paragraph (not in block format), but provide slash marks to show where her original lines were broken, as in the following example:

In her poem "Diving into the Wreck," Adrienne Rich assumes that our history of the past is a largely fictionalized "book of myths," a metaphoric place that is dangerous for the female explorer because historians have traditionally neglected the actions of women in their accounts of our past (line 1). To document what really occurred in history, she "loaded the camera" to record the events, she "checked the edge of the knife-blade" that she might need to protect herself or to pry beneath superficial appearances, and she put on "the body-armor of black rubber / the absurd flippers / the grave and awkward mask" (2, 3, 5–7). To Rich, exploring the past is a dangerous but valuable enterprise that requires much preparation.

This paragraph illustrates much of the same selection and introduction of the quoted material that I discussed earlier. The relevant phrases have all been grammatically worked into the author's own phrasing, so that all the words, quoted and original, produce grammatical and coherent sentences. When the quoted lines break in the original, those breaks have been marked with spaced slash marks. Marking such breaks in this fashion is important only in quoting lines of poetry within your regular text, and failure to do so ignores an important feature of the original poem.

QUOTATION MARKS AND OTHER PUNCTUATION

Below are some more examples that illustrate a variety of punctuation circumstances.

A semicolon following a quotation:
Nick calls Gatsby's guests "moths"; perhaps he is not so impartial after all.

A colon following a quotation:
Emma cited several reasons for what she called her "unrestrained rage": Cathy's arrogance, Tom's indifference, and Jackie's boredom.

A quotation with an exclamation point and parenthetical page number:
The technician said, "That lapse in procedure is inexcusable!" (16).

A quotation with an exclamation point followed by attribution:
"That lapse in procedure is inexcusable!" said the technician (16).

A quoted question:
The task force sought to answer one question: "Why did the bridge collapse?"

A quoted question and parenthetical page number:
In *The Culture of Fear*, Barry Glassner asks, "Why, as crime rates plunged throughout the 1990s, did two-thirds of Americans believe they were soaring?" (xi).

A quoted phrase that is part of a question you ask:
At what point did the corporation become entirely self-serving and no longer a "public institution whose purpose was to serve national interests and advance the public good" (Bakan 153)?

HOW SHOULD YOU SELECT AND CITE ELECTRONIC AND INTERNET SOURCES?

The Internet and the proliferation of other electronic and online resources have made information more readily available than ever before. But the variety of such materials has also greatly increased the need for you to critically assess the information you find. The ease with which you can move from site to site, click on links, shrink and open new windows, and cut and paste information to notepads or to documents—this rapid movement from source to source practically *encourages* sloppy and unethical uses of copyrighted information and wording. The format of the Web creates the dangerous illusion that the items you find on it are free and/or public property, akin to common knowledge that isn't owned by an author. Unlike printed material in a library, the information on an electronic source is subject to frequent change, and if you haven't been careful to copy all of the information you will need at the time you see it (or better yet, printed a hard copy of the page), you might lose your access to it, if the text has been revised. A Web page might not even list an author's name, and a particular page to which you might have been linked might not present any publishing information or context for the material on your screen.

Browsing the Web seems like—and often *is*—a form of leisurely entertainment, and your habits during recreation can have dire consequences if they spill over into your writing and suspend the careful sorts of critical thinking and responsible note-taking that are essential to responsible professional and academic writing. Further, the visual similarities among different kinds of documents, when all are filtered through a browser or computer, tend to blur distinctions among them, to make them all seem equal in their reliability or authority. But there are extreme differences among the kinds of material you can view online. Despite all of these challenges, you can learn to sort the nonsense and idiocy from the truly relevant and reputable, and you can use the information with the same scrutiny and care that persuasive writers learn to apply to all that they read.

Much of the early praise for the potential of the Internet focused on the freedom of access to it as a means of publishing—as if the Internet represented the full realization of a democracy in which all people could publish and read virtually everything. At a local level, that freedom takes the form of policies of many Internet service providers that grant all subscribers some space on the server to launch their own websites. In effect, anyone who subscribes to an Internet service may post information.

One practical effect of this accessibility is that the millions of documents and images available from a terminal represent a complete mix of wholly valuable and reputable information with information that is biased, deceptive, or totally unimportant. With careful attention to the source, meticulous critical assessment of evidence and authority, and some detective work, you may find highly useful and credible information related to your topic. For example, major newspapers, magazines, and news organizations usually have websites—often electronic editions of or supplements to their publications and broadcasts. When you know the agency or organization that hosts the site, and the site has been assembled with the same care and editorial standards as the organization's other work, you may rely on the website with as much confidence as you would the print publication or broadcast.

Intermixed with online journals are countless commercial sites, individuals' Web pages and blogs, university sites, government sites, nonprofit agency pages, and highly varied other electronic forums for exchange of information. A United States government electronic archive of Senate hearings might be a click or two away from a child's hobby page. Readings posted on the Web by a professor might seem to blend seamlessly with essays written by her students. Always consider the source. The nature of your topic will assist you in determining if a particular site is relevant to your project.

SOURCE RELIABILITY: A SAMPLE TOPIC

An example will illustrate a few of the challenges involved in assessing the reliability of websites. Suppose you are writing an essay on the proposal to permit exploratory drilling for oil in Alaska's Arctic National Wildlife Refuge (ANWR). Entering "ANWR oil exploration" in any of the large Internet search engines (Yahoo, for example) will yield links to many related sites. The sheer variety of them should suggest that you need to choose a highly precise focus to make the topic manageable in an essay. That proposal involves issues of natural resource preservation, the international oil market, national security, electoral politics, ecological effects (themselves a highly varied lot), effects on other regional industries (like salmon), anthropological concerns, and a host of other issues. If your topic is any one of these, you will need to sift through contentious and contradictory claims by the involved parties: the oil corporations, the political figures (national and state), interest groups (on many sides), scientists, economists, lawyers, indigenous peoples, labor unions, and environmentalists. Many of these sources will simply be too biased by self-interest to serve as reputable authorities. But if your essay focuses on the conduct of the arguments themselves, on the *rhetoric* of some focused aspect of the debate, then virtually any of these sources could become primary material. The language and argument employed by various parties could become your topic as they illustrate various techniques of argument and propaganda.

A fifteen-minute search of the topic reveals that the national interest in this proposal has energized public relations efforts on the part of industry and environmental groups—to name just two general sides in the debate. The sophistication of such efforts complicates one's attempts to find balanced discussions of the topic—at least on Internet sites. The well-funded participants in this debate have learned the advantages of paying for prominence in the search engine results. Many of the links that appear among the first ten on Google or Yahoo have not been selected by an impartial search program according to their relevance. Google and Yahoo are commercial sites that sell those positions. You will need to search with varied keywords and scroll through many pages of results to find different perspectives. There is certainly no correlation between a site's placement in the search results and its reliability as an authority for research purposes.

You should pay attention to the URL domain of the sites you find—the kind of abbreviation that follows the dot, whether com, net, org, edu, or gov. The advocacy groups—whether for the oil industry or for environmental concerns—realize that readers are rightly suspicious of sites with a .com domain, as this signifies the for-profit purpose of the site. So they've formed organizations or connections with universities that permit them to use .org and .edu domains. On a politically charged topic like oil exploration in Alaska, it might also be the case that United States government sites (with .gov domains) are urging particular policies or legislative initiatives. The management of public information is, of course, a strategic effort—one that may or may not yield reliable information with a basis in fact. Little is as it appears to be in the cyberspace battle for public opinion. Remaining skeptical, seeking evidence of bias or agenda, and being persistent in identifying the members and missions of organizations will be crucial whenever you're looking at Web resources on complicated, hot national topics.

Most of the websites discussing Alaskan oil exploration foreground their credibility in sometimes transparent ways. For example, one site, called simply ANWR.org, describes its parent organization, Arctic Power, as a "grassroots, non-profit citizen's organization with 10,000 members founded in April of 1992 . . ." ("About Us," ANWR.org). The organization emphasizes how comprehensive its membership is:

> Arctic Power membership spans the economic spectrum—including miners, fishermen, loggers, tourism operators, transportation businesses, labor unions, banks, teachers, the legal community, retail firms, service industries, non-profit organizations, Alaska Native corporations, local elected officials, and many others. ("About Us," ANWR.org)

The prominent links on its home page certainly make it seem as if it's got this complicated issue covered, attending to veterans, labor, Alaskans, and even caribou. But all of these topics are discussed with one mission in mind: "to expedite congressional and presidential approval of oil exploration and production within the Coastal Plain of the Arctic National Wildlife Refuge" ("About Us," ANWR.org). The board of directors for Arctic Power includes representatives of the Alaska Support Industry Alliance, the Alaska State Chamber of Commerce, the Resource Development

Council, the Alaska Miner's Association, and the Alaska Oil & Gas Association. On the one hand, having such members on its board gives the group insight into corporate positions on the issue. On the other, it casts doubt on the extent to which the group is truly a "grassroots" movement, representing a citizen's initiative. Its site offers brief arguments, sometimes called *talking points*, in quick tours of the topic. The rhetoric of the site is a mix of seeming neutrality and energetically partisan advocacy. Like other oil industry–funded groups with .org domains, this one works to gain credibility as a moderate group with broad support, and then engages in passionate and one-sided argument.

Similar strategies are employed by groups opposing exploratory drilling in Alaska, as well. One such group, the Alaska Coalition, describes itself as a coalition of "[n]early 1000 conservation, sporting, labor and religious groups working together to protect our public lands in Alaska" ("About Us," Alaska Coalition). Claiming to be born of cooperation among nearly a thousand organizations with highly varied missions, the Coalition offers an organizational self-portrait drawn with many of the same strokes as those of Arctic Power: cooperation, diversity, and populism. And like the site of Arctic Power, the Coalition's site offers talking points, links to other activist groups, and calls for action and public support—but for conservation, not drilling. There are sites more oriented toward information than bandwagon activism, such as one maintained by Ecotrust calling itself Inforain and providing a survey of research and analysis ("About Us," Inforain). Though this site is better documented, calmer, and far more substantive than the Coalition's site, it is very much a pro-conservation site and therefore a partisan in the debate.

When you choose a topic fraught with controversy, you need to seek varied points of view and pay meticulous attention to the sorts of evidence provided by the sources and the overall validity of the reasoning they employ. Check the credentials of the principal authors, and attempt to verify the information they provide by consulting additional sources, ideally universities, major news organizations, print publications (ones without economic ties to the interested parties), government documents, and court reports. As this sample topic illustrates, you should be cautious and skeptical of all claims—doubly so when the source is online. The Web has evolved into an enterprise that is chiefly commercial. You should not limit your research to Internet sites, unless such texts are well suited to your topic.

CITING INTERNET WEBSITES

Citing paraphrased or quoted information from Internet sources requires some adaptation of your usual procedures. If you know the name of the author or of the organization, name it in your text as you introduce the material, mentioning the publication medium as you do so (website, CD-ROM, online journal, and so forth). If you need to cite a particular page from a website, place the title of the page in quotation marks in parentheses at the end of the sentence. Titles of pages or sections within sites are often quite long, and quoting them in your text in their entirety would be cumbersome. In such cases, you need to preserve the first word of the section name (to enable your readers to easily identify it among your list of works cited) and then use an abbreviated or shortened form that refers to the full citation in your list. Writing an abbreviated title isn't always a simple matter. For example, a link on the Natural Resources Defense Council home page is entitled "Big Oil Is Destroying Our Greatest Songbird Nursery." The page itself, if you click on that link, is headed "Stop the Pipeline! Save Our Songbirds." In this case, the best thing might be simply to use "Stop the Pipeline!" making certain that the actual full citation is clear in your list of works cited. When you determine how to refer to a source, make certain that your parenthetical citation includes the first detail in the works cited entry for the source—the words according to which the source has been positioned alphabetically in your list. The format for listing websites will differ according to the appropriate style manual for your discipline. And, because the kinds of sources continue to evolve, most of the style manuals offer only provisional guidance and admit that the guidelines will be changing as the media evolve. But nearly all of the formats require that your final list include the author or organization (if known), the title of the page, the latest date that the page was updated (if known), and the date you actually consulted it.

The convenience of consulting websites has two costs: the need to be particularly alert to various ways the sites might be unreliable, and the challenges of citing sometimes tricky documents. It's not always easy to tell who the author is, and you might not find a date that the document was last revised—though you should explore other links on the home page to try to find this information. You may not know whether a title should be presented as a part of a whole (and placed in quotation marks) or as a site on its own (and underlined or italicized). Remember to consult the latest edition of the style manual for the discipline in which you are writing. The most recent format guides by the different professional organizations indicate that there is continuing disagreement about what kinds of information are required for citing Internet sites. MLA has decided not to require the URL (Universal Resource Locator) but to require indicating the medium of all sources cited (Web and Print, primarily). Some formats require the date you gained access to the material on the Web; others do not. Some sample citations illustrating the main differences in format are printed in the next chapter.

OTHER ELECTRONIC SOURCES

Your computer might be linked to some databases to which your university or employer subscribes. Because you gain access to these databases with your Internet browser, they might seem like ordinary websites, but they are actually distinct from the Internet. One such database is *LexisNexis*, frequently available on campuses. *LexisNexis* offers searchable, computerized archives of published documents. This powerful—and expensive—service is a highly useful means of gaining access to electronic versions of materials originally published in a variety of media: newspapers, magazines, journals, newsletters, trade publications, and abstracts. *LexisNexis* enables you to view and print information directly from your computer without the need to find the printed source in a library. It provides the actual written texts from the original sources but without the graphics, visual layout, and pagination of the originals. Generally believed to be reputably edited and reliable texts, the items found on *LexisNexis* are really distinct versions of the original works. The service does provide the full publication information for the items, but it reformats the document in ways that do not enable you to tell on which page in the document a given sentence or paragraph appears. Because the item has been significantly reformatted from its original form, you must cite the version you consulted, indicating that the material was obtained through *LexisNexis*. Presumably, the actual words have been presented accurately by the editors, but the authority for the accuracy of that transcription now resides at *LexisNexis*. Your citation should indicate that the online service owns the version you consulted and that what you cite is at one stage of removal from the original printed text.

When consulting such an archive, you need to make yourself familiar with how it works—both with how the search engine enables you to make choices among dates and kinds of materials and with how the service organizes and labels the parts of the original citation. The author's name might be called the "byline"; the title of an article might be called the "headline." The services offer guidance and tips that enable you to figure out how the original citation would be reconstructed from what they provide, and most include a link to some sample citations following various formats. When you cite in your regular text a source obtained through one of these services, use the author's name (if available) or the title, as you would if you were citing the original version. This reference, whether explicit or parenthetical, should clearly identify to which item in your list of works cited the name refers. Unless the service provides the original page numbers, you do not provide them. In your list of works cited, begin by citing the work as you would the original, and then follow it by noting either the title of the online service or the URL for the site, according to the required format. Consult the appropriate style manual for your discipline for the exact way of listing such a source. If you've found an item on a service such as *LexisNexis* and not consulted the original version, you must not cite it without acknowledging the online source.

Other subscription databases that are frequently available at libraries include *InfoTrac* (by Thomson Learning), *Academic Search Complete* and *Business Source Complete* (by EBSCOhost), and *ProQuest*. Like *LexisNexis*, these databases present the full texts of documents but reformat them in ways that do not preserve the original layout and pagination. Because the original page number for a passage will not be identified by these databases, parenthetical citations to such sources usually will consist of only the author's name. The entry in the list of works cited must acknowledge that the version of the document you consulted was provided by the database. The URL for the actual document is probably long and complicated, often a series of symbols and letters that is a temporary designation. For this reason, if you need to provide the URL, list the URL for the database, not the one for the document itself.

If the database provides scanned images of the original pages of the publication, as is sometimes done with articles from scholarly journals, then you should provide the page number in your parenthetical citation as you normally would. In your works cited, you still must cite the online archive or service that provided the scanned image. *JSTOR* (Journal Storage) is one such archive. Operated by a nonprofit organization, the *JSTOR* collection spans nearly every discipline and is continually expanding. It typically does not include current issues of scholarly publications. There is likely to be a gap of several years between the most recent issue and those included in the archive. The *JSTOR* archive greatly expands the availability of scholarly journals and the ease with which they may be consulted. It is crucial that you acknowledge the archive as you cite sources obtained with it—not only to be academically honest but also to support the service.

Below are some citations of documents from subscription databases in MLA format.

Barash, Jeffrey Andrew. "The Sources of Memory." *Journal of the History of Ideas* 58 (1997): 707–17. *JSTOR*. Web. 2 Aug. 2010.

"Consumers Consider the Importance of Corporate Social Responsibility." *Strategic Finance*, August 2006: 20–22. *Business Source Complete*. Web.10 July 2010.

Dunn, Joseph. "How Electric Cars Came Back from the Dead." *Sunday Times (London)*, 23 July 2006: 6. *LexisNexis*. Web. 6 Aug. 2010.

Livingstone, Sonia, and Ellen J. Helsper. "Does Advertising Literacy Mediate the Effects of Advertising on Children? A Critical Examination of Two Linked Research Literatures in Relation to Obesity and Food Choice." *Journal of Communication* 56 (2006): 560–84. *Academic Search Complete*. Web. 6 Aug. 2006.

Don't despair if at first all of these rules seem complicated. Much of this material is probably review, and all of it will become second nature to you with practice. The procedures for quoting and paraphrasing are vitally important, even if they strike you at first as merely cosmetic or surface details. Following these conventions will reassure your readers that you are ethical, competent, and careful. And if all of the papers you write are put in proper form before you turn them in, you free your professor to comment on the substance of what you say—things that probably both of you find more interesting. After all, your professor has only a limited amount of space and time to devote to commenting on your writing, and if your paper is in poor form, you waste valuable time that could be spent on more interesting matters.

Keep this book and refer to it whenever your memory of these conventions fades. Chapter 9 provides a brief checklist. You should consult it while revising papers that employ quoted or paraphrased material.

A FURTHER NOTE
ABOUT STYLE
MANUALS

Unless you have already chosen a major or a field of specialization, it doesn't make sense for you to purchase the standard style manual for every course you take in different fields. Most writing handbooks include enough information about the major style manuals to suffice in introductory classes. Once you are committed to a field of study, however, it is important for you to purchase the manual that your professor or advisor recommends for that field. You will discover that many of the features of manuscript form, some of the features of writing style, and the format for both in-text citations and for lists of references at the end of a work differ from one field to the next in significant ways. Learning to apply the guidelines for your field is part of learning the field. It might seem as if the differences from one field to the next are tiny, and they might seem arbitrary or merely a matter of a teacher's preference. But the guidelines are not, in fact, arbitrary. They reflect the values and methods of inquiry characteristic of the field to which they apply. For example, when formats in the natural sciences seem to emphasize the year of publication, it makes sense because the recentness of information in the natural sciences typically matters more than it might in the humanities. If the natural sciences are meticulous about citing all the authors of a multi-author work, it makes sense because so many research projects involve collaborative or team efforts. You might not always know the reasons for features of the prescribed formats, but your work will appear more mature and professional if you care about and apply the guidelines in the appropriate style manual.

Below are some sample citations, included here only to illustrate a few of the differences among some prominent styles.

AN ARTICLE IN A MAGAZINE

MLA (*MLA Handbook for Writers of Research Papers*)
Gottlieb, Lori. "How to Land Your Kid in Therapy." *Atlantic Monthly* July–Aug. 2011: 64–78. Print.

CMS (*Chicago Manual of Style*)
Gottlieb, Lori. "How to Land Your Kid in Therapy." *Atlantic Monthly*, July/August 2011, 64–78.

CSE (*Scientific Style and Format*)
Gottlieb L. 2011 Jul–Aug. How to land your kid in therapy. *Atlantic Monthly*: 64–78.

APA (*Publication Manual of the American Psychological Association*)
Gottlieb, L. (2011, July/August). How to land your kid in therapy. *Atlantic Monthly*, 64–78.

ACS (*The ACS Style Guide*)
Gottlieb, L. How to Land Your Kid in Therapy. *Atlantic*, July/Aug, 2011, pp 64–78.

APSA (*Style Manual for Political Science*)
Gottlieb, Lori. 2011. "How to Land Your Kid in Therapy." *Atlantic Monthly*, July/Aug, 64–78.

A BOOK

MLA
Shuler, Jack. *Calling Out Liberty: The Stono Slave Rebellion and the Universal Struggle for Human Rights*. Jackson, MS: UP of Mississippi, 2009. Print.

CMS
Shuler, Jack. *Calling Out Liberty: The Stono Slave Rebellion and the Universal Struggle for Human Rights*. Jackson, MS: University Press of Mississippi, 2009.

CSE
Shuler J. 2009. Calling out liberty: the Stono slave rebellion and the universal struggle for human rights. Jackson, MS: UP of Mississippi. 217 p.

APA
Shuler, J. (2009). *Calling Out Liberty: The Stono Slave Rebellion and the Universal Struggle for Human Rights*. Jackson, MS: UP of Mississippi.

ACS
Shuler, J. *Calling Out Liberty: The Stono Slave Rebellion and the Universal Struggle for Human Rights*. UP of Mississippi: Jackson, MS, 2009.

APSA
Shuler, Jack. 2009. *Calling Out Liberty: The Stono Slave Rebellion and the Universal Struggle for Human Rights*. Jackson, MS: UP of Mississippi.

A WEBSITE

MLA

Sierra Club. Sierra Club, 2011. Web. 1 July 2011.

CMS

Sierra Club. *Sierra Club.* http://www.sierraclub.org/.

CSE

Sierra Club home page [Internet]. San Francisco, CA: Sierra Club; 2011 [cited 2011 July 1]. Available from: http://www .sierraclub.org/.

APA

Sierra Club. (2011). *Sierra Club Home Page.* Retrieved from http://www.sierraclub.org/

ACS

Sierra Club Home Page. http://www.sierraclub.org/ (accessed July 1, 2001).

APSA

Sierra Club. 2011. *Sierra Club Home Page.* http://www.sierra club.org/(July 1, 2011).

A PUBLISHED ARTICLE FROM AN ONLINE DATABASE

MLA

Francia, Peter L. "Campaign Finance after *Citizens United:* What the Future May Hold." *Campaigns & Elections* May 2011: 16–18. *Academic Search Complete.* Web. 1 July 2011.

CMS

Francia, Peter L. "Campaign Finance after *Citizens United*: What the Future May Hold." *Campaigns & Elections*, May 2011: 16–18. http://search.ebscohost.com/.

CSE

Francia PL. 2011 May. Campaign finance after Citizens United: what the future may hold. Campaigns & elections: 16–18. [cited 2011 July 1]. Available from: http://search.ebscohost .com/.

APA

Francia, P. (2011, May). Campaign finance after *Citizens United*: What the future may hold. *Campaigns & Elections*, 16–18. Retrieved from http://search.ebscohost.com/

ACS

Francia, P. Campaign Finance after *Citizens United*: What the Future May Hold. *Campaigns & Elections*, May, 2011, pp 16–18. Academic Source Complete. http://search.ebscohos t.com/ (accessed July 1, 2011).

APSA

Francia, Peter L. 2011. "Campaign Finance after Citizens United: What the Future May Hold." *Campaigns & Elections*, May, 64–68. http:search.ebscohost.com/ (accessed July 1, 2011).

REVISION CHECKLIST FOR QUOTING AND PARAPHRASING

1. Are all of your paragraphs developed adequately, with evidence for your argument or illustration of your complex ideas? Is the paragraph primarily your words, with quotations or paraphrased evidence serving only as supporting material? Do you provide too much information from sources, or too little?
2. If you have paraphrased, did you introduce the material from your source to indicate clearly what is from the source? Did you mention the author? Did you provide a note or a parenthetical citation of the source so that your readers would have all the information they need to locate the source and page from which the information comes?
3. Is the wording of paraphrased material entirely your own? Does it accurately reflect the viewpoint expressed in the original?
4. If you quote, have you introduced each passage, or does your context make it clear that the words are quoted from a source? Have you followed the quotation with a page number or with a note? Is each quoted passage introduced sufficiently so that quoted words fit together grammatically

with your own, to ensure that your reader will understand the significance of the passage?

5. Are quoted words in proper form? Are they quoted accurately and marked by quotation marks? Have any added words or letters been placed in square brackets, and have deleted words been replaced by an ellipsis? Have you indicated the line breaks in quoted poetry with slash marks? Have you punctuated the quotations properly?

6. Have you followed all quotations, particularly longer, block quotations, with your own analysis or interpretation of the passages? Are the transitions to and from quoted material smooth and coherent?

7. If you've consulted sources that have been indexed and re-presented by an online database, have you noted the online version that you have cited?

8. Have you followed the format for citations required by the style manual that is used in your discipline? Do all of your citations present all of the necessary information about the works you consulted?

APPENDIX:
INTERNET RESOURCES

This section presents useful websites organized by disciplines within the humanities and social sciences. Some of these sites provide resources for research within a discipline, and some provide guides for writing papers and citing sources. Each discipline has its own resources and its own rules, so these sites provide an introduction to these resources and rules. They barely scratch the surface of what's available on the Internet, but they should provide a good start.

ANTHROPOLOGY

American Anthropological Association Resources on the Internet
AAA's list of links of interest to anthropologists.
   http://www.aaanet.org/resources/

Anthropology in the News
Contains the latest findings throughout anthropology. Maintained by Texas A&M University.
   http://anthropology.tamu.edu/news/

Society of American Archaeology Links

This site has a list of references for archaeologists and archaeology students.

http://saa.org/publicftp/PUBLIC/resources/resources.html

Voice of the Shuttle: Anthropology and Archaeology Pages

These sites have references to a wide range of current writings from anthropologists and archaeologists, as well as general resources.
http://vos.ucsb.edu

The World Wide Web Virtual Library: Social and Behavioral Sciences

General resource with links for disciplines within the social sciences.

http://vlib.org/SocialSciences

COMMUNICATION

Handouts and Links: Communications

Describes steps for planning and writing papers in communications studies courses, with links to other writing resources, at The Writing Center, University of North Carolina, Chapel Hill.
http://www.unc.edu/depts/wcweb/handouts/communications
.html

National Speakers Association

Resources for speakers, whether professional or amateur.
http://www.nsaspeaker.org

Online Communication Studies Resources

This site contains an index of online resources for communication studies, including advertising, film studies, and political communication. Maintained by the Department of Communication Studies at the University of Iowa.

http://www.uiowa.edu/commstud/resources/about.html

Political Communication Resources

A gateway to Internet sites containing useful information about the media and democracy, created by Lance Bennett.
http://depts.washington.edu/bennett/

Toastmasters International

Resources for making speeches from Toastmasters International.
http://www.toastmasters.org/MainMenuCategories/Free Resources.aspx

Voice of the Shuttle: Media Studies Page

This site has references to a wide range of current writings from media studies scholars, as well as general resources.
http://vos.ucsb.edu

ENGLISH AND COMPOSITION

Elements of Style

The online version of the popular English composition handbook.
http://www.bartleby.com/141

EServer Rhetoric and Composition

Links to resources in rhetoric and composition.
http://www.rhetoric.eserver.org

Modern Language Association

Official website of the MLA. Includes a section on frequently asked questions about MLA style as well as links to resources and publications.
http://www.mla.org

The OWL at Purdue

An online writing lab offering free writing help and teaching resources. Maintained by Purdue University.
http://owl.english.purdue.edu

Resources for Writers and Writing Instructors
Links to a number of writing resources, maintained by Jack Lynch
at Rutgers University.
http://andromeda.rutgers.edu/~jlynch/Writing/links.html

Writing@CSU
Home of Colorado State University's online learning environment, the Writing Studio. Use this site to learn to write, save
your work in a private password-protected account, and get
feedback on your writing.
http://writing.colostate.edu

FILM STUDIES

American Film Institute
AFI is a national institute providing leadership in screen education.
http://www.afi.com

Dartmouth Writing Program
Features tips for writing about film.
http://www.dartmouth.edu/~writing/materials/student/
humanities/film.shtml

The Internet Movie Database
An award-winning movie website that includes reviews of current
movies, message boards, and a vast database of films.
http://www.imdb.com

Movie Review Query Engine
A guide to film reviews.
http://www.mrqe.com

GEOGRAPHY

About Geography
A list of current articles on geography in the news, as well as general resources.
http://geography.about.com

Internet Resources for Geographers
General resources for geography. Maintained by the Department of Geography at the University of Colorado, Boulder.
http://www.colorado.edu/geography/virtdept/resources/contents.htm

Internet Resources for Geography and Geology
General resources for geography and geology. Maintained by the University of Wisconsin, Stevens Point.
http://www.uwsp.edu/geo/internet/geog_geol_resources.html

Map Projections Poster
Map projections resources maintained by the U.S. Geological Survey.
http://library.usgs.gov/maplinks.html

MAPS AND CARTOGRAPHY

Earth Science and Map Library Map Collection at the University of California, Berkeley
http://www.lib.berkeley.edu/EART/MapCollections.html

New Books in Geography
A list of new books in geography. Maintained by the Association of American Geographers.
http://www.aag.org/cs/publications/new_books_in_geography/new_books_from_earthscan

HISTORY

Dartmouth Writing Program

A student guide to writing a history paper, provided by Dartmouth College.

http://www.dartmouth.edu/~writing/materials/student/soc_
sciences/history.shtml

History Matters

History Matters serves as a gateway to Web resources and offers other useful materials for teaching U.S. history.

http://historymatters.gmu.edu

History Writing Guides

Guide to reading and interpreting primary sources. Very helpful for researchers.

http://academic.bowdoin.edu/WritingGuides

History and Theory

This website and online journal is devoted to exploring the links between philosophy and history.

http://www.historyandtheory.org

Voice of the Shuttle: History Page

This site has references to a wide range of writings from world historians, as well as general resources.

http://vos.ucsb.edu

Women's Biographies: Distinguished Women of Past and Present

This site is devoted to the history of women throughout the world.

http://www.DistinguishedWomen.com

World History Matters

World History Matters is a portal to world history links on the Web.

http://worldhistorymatters.org

The World Wide Web Virtual Library: History Index

General resource with links to many history resources. Maintained by the University of Kansas.

http://vlib.iue.it/history

JOURNALISM

The Associated Press Style Book

An important style guide for all popular publications. People who do public relations and advertising generally follow AP style as well in their writing. It is also a good guide for general writing.

http://www.apstylebook.com

Association for Education in Journalism and Mass Communication Links

A list of links to appropriate, noncommercial websites of interest to members of the Association for Education in Journalism and Mass Communication.

http://www.aejmc.org/_scholarship/_publications/_resources/index.php

JournalismNet

JournalismNet is an extensive list of resources for journalists, including daily news updates.

http://www.journalismnet.com

The Journalist's Toolbox

The Journalist's Toolbox contains links to areas of interest to journalists, as well as teaching tools for editors and professors. Maintained by the Society for Professional Journalists.

http://www.journaliststoolbox.org/

The Poynter Center

A resource for writing about news and current affairs.

http://poynter.org

Project for Excellence in Journalism: Understanding News in the Information Age

The website of the Project for Excellence in Journalism, a research organization that specializes in using empirical methods to evaluate and study the performance of the press. Features news and links to other resources.

http://www.journalism.org

Society of Professional Journalists

The website of the Society of Professional Journalists, a large and broad-based national journalism organization.

http://spj.org

PHILOSOPHY

The American Philosophical Association's Web Resources

A list of philosophical associations and societies, centers and institutes, and electronic texts. Maintained by the American Philosophical Association.

http://apaonline.org/resources/index.aspx

Dartmouth Writing Program

A student guide to writing a philosophy paper, provided by Dartmouth College.

http://www.dartmouth.edu/~writing/materials/student/humanities/philosophy.shtml

Descartes' Meditations Home Page

This site contains an online edition of Descartes' classic work of philosophical reflections.

http://www.wright.edu/cola/descartes

Ethics Updates Home Page

This site contains resources on the following topics: moral theory, relativism, pluralism, religion, and egoism.

http://ethics.sandiego.edu

Philosophers: Main Page
This site provides easy access to resources in philosophy, categorized by philosopher.
http://www.epistemelinks.com/Main/MainPers.asp

Philosophy News Service
A list of contemporary news in philosophy.
http://www.philosophynews.com/

Philosophy Pages
This site focuses on Web links to Western philosophy sites, created by Garth Kemerling.
http://www.philosophypages.com/

Philosophy, Introduction
This site provides a general overview of what philosophy is.
http://pespmc1.vub.ac.be/PHILOSI.html

Stanford Encyclopedia of Philosophy
An extensive online encyclopedia of philosophy.
http://plato.stanford.edu

Voice of the Shuttle: Philosophy Page
This site has references to a wide range of writings from philosophers, as well as general resources.
http://vos.ucsb.edu

POLITICAL SCIENCE

Inter-university Consortium for Political and Social Research Front Page
This site contains social science data and resources for researchers.
http://www.icpsr.umich.edu/

Resources for Political Science

A list of political science organizations, research in progress, and upcoming publications. Maintained by the American Political Science Association.

http://apsanet.org/section_188.cfm

Voice of the Shuttle: Politics and Government Page

This site has references to a wide range of writings from scholars of politics and government, as well as general resources.

http://vos.ucsb.edu

RELIGION

AAR Other Resources

The American Academy of Religion's list of other resources for religious studies scholars.

http://www.aarweb.org/About_AAR/Related_Organizations/default.asp

Dartmouth Writing Program

A student guide to writing a religion paper, provided by Dartmouth College.

http://www.dartmouth.edu/~writing/materials/student/humanities/religion.shtml

Voice of the Shuttle: Religious Studies Page

This site has references to a wide range of general religious studies resources, as well as links to sites dedicated to the thinkings of many major religious and spiritual groups.

http://vos.ucsb.edu

SOCIOLOGY

American Sociological Association Manuscript Checklist

http://www2.asanet.org/pubs/asaguidelinesnew.pdf

Classical Sociological Theory
This site contains online texts of classical social thinkers. Maintained by the University of Chicago.
http://ssr1.uchicago.edu/PRELIMS/theory.html

Dartmouth Writing Program
A student guide to writing a sociology paper, provided by Dartmouth College.
http://www.dartmouth.edu/~writing/materials/student/soc_sciences/sociology.shtml

Online Communication Studies Resources
This site contains an index of online resources for cultural studies. Maintained by the Department of Communication Studies at the University of Iowa.
http://www.uiowa.edu/commstud/resources/about.html

Social Science Hub
Excellent starting point for research. Comprehensive enough to include many of the major categories within the discipline.
http://mediaresearchhub.ssrc.org/

SociologyOnline
This British site for all students of sociology, criminology, and social thought is full of information about both classical and contemporary thinkers.
http://www.sociologyonline.co.uk/

SocioSite
This site, maintained by the University of Amsterdam, provides a global perspective on sociology with access to a number of European theorists.
http://www.sociosite.net/index.php

Voice of the Shuttle: Cultural Studies Page
This site has references to a wide range of current sociological thinkers, many specifically oriented toward cultural theories.
http://vos.ucsb.edu

WORKS CITED

"About Us." *Alaska Coalition*. Alaska Coalition. 2011. Web. 1 July 2011.

"About Us." *ANWR.org: Jobs and Energy for America*. Arctic Power. 2011. Web. 1 July 2011.

"About Us." *Inforain*. Ecotrust. 2011. Web. 1 July 2011.

Arden, John Boghosian. *America's Meltdown: The Lowest-Common-De-nominator Society*. Westport, CT: Praeger, 2003. Print.

"Astroturf." *SourceWatch: Your Guide to the Names behind the News*. Center for Media and Democracy. 15 May 2011. Web. 31 May 2011.

Bakan, Joel. *The Corporation: The Pathological Pursuit of Profit and Power*. New York: Free Press, 2004. Print.

Baker, Russ. "The Squeeze: Some Major Advertisers Step Up the Pressure on Magazines to Alter Their Content. Will Editors Bend?" *Columbia Journalism Review* Sept./Oct. 1997: 30–36. *LexisNexis Academic Universe*. Web. 14 Mar. 2005.

Blake, William. "The Chimney Sweeper." *The Norton Anthology of English Literature: The Major Authors*. 8th ed. Ed. Stephen Greenblatt et al. New York: Norton, 2006. 1414. Print.

Brisbane, Arthur S. "Scholarly Work, Without All the Footnotes." Editorial. *New York Times*. New York Times, 2 Oct. 2010. Web. 3 Oct. 2010.

Carson, Rachel. *The Silent Spring*. Cambridge, MA: Riverside Press, 1962. Print.

Falk, William. "Should Old Articles Be Forgot." *New York Times.* New York Times, 29 Dec. 2009. Web. 30 Dec. 2009.

Fitzgerald, F. Scott. *The Great Gatsby.* New York: Charles Scribner's Sons, 1925. Print.

Foster, Andrea L. "Information Navigation 101." *Chronicle of Higher Education.* Chronicle of Higher Education, 9 Mar. 2007. Web. 7 Aug. 2009.

Gladwell, Malcolm. "Big and Bad: How the S.U.V. Ran Over Automotive Safety." *New Yorker* 12 Jan. 2004: 28–33. Print.

Glassner, Barry. *The Culture of Fear: Why Americans Are Afraid of the Wrong Things.* New York: Basic Books, 1999. Print.

Gray, Kathy Lynn. "OU Tells 37 Grads to Redo Theses: Cheating as High as 84% by Undergrads, Campus Survey Finds." *Columbus Dispatch.* Columbus Dispatch, 22 July 2006. Web. 24 July 2006.

Hafner, Katie. "Seeing Corporate Fingerprints in Wikipedia Edits." *New York Times.* New York Times, 19 Aug. 2007. Web. 19 Aug. 2007.

Hesse, Monica. "Truth: Can You Handle It?" *Washingtonpost.com.* Washington Post, 27 Apr. 2008. Web. 5 May 2008.

Klein, Naomi. *No Logo.* New York: Picador, 2000. Print.

Manjoo, Farhad. *True Enough: Learning to Live in a Post-Fact Society.* Hoboken, NJ: Wiley, 2008. Print.

"On Compromise, Great Expectations, and Asking the Tough Questions: Excerpts from Graduation Speeches." *Chronicle of Higher Education.* Chronicle of Higher Education, 20 June 2010. Web. 23 May 2011.

Quinn, Carin C. "The Jeaning of America—and the World." *American Heritage* Apr./May 1978: 14–21. Print.

Rich, Adrienne. "Diving into the Wreck." *The Fact of a Doorframe: Selected Poems 1950–2001.* New York: W. W. Norton, 2002. Print.

Rich, Frank. "Facebook Politicians Are Not Your Friends." Editorial. *New York Times.* New York Times, 9 Oct. 2010. Web. 10 Oct. 2010.

"SourceWatch: Purpose." *SourceWatch: Your Guide to the Names behind the News.* Center for Media and Democracy. 17 Apr. 2010. Web. 31 May 2011.

Stelter, Brian. "Debunkers of Fictions Sift the Net." *New York Times.* New York Times, 4 Apr. 2010. Web. 5 Apr. 2010.

"Stop the Pipeline! Save Our Songbirds." *NRDC*. Natural Resources Defense Council. 2011. Web. 1 July 2011.

Strogatz, Steven. "Fibbing with Numbers." Rev. of *Proofiness: The Dark Arts of Mathematical Deception*, by Charles Seife. *New York Times: Sunday Book Review*. New York Times, 17 Sept. 2010. Web. 3 June 2011.

Sullivan, John. "True Enough: The Second Age of PR." *Columbia Journalism Review* May/June 2011: 34–39. Print.

Young, Jeffrey R. "High-Tech Cheating Abounds, and Professors Bear Some Blame." *Chronicle of Higher Education*. Chronicle of Higher Education, 28 Mar. 2010. Web. 29 Mar. 2010.

ABOUT THE AUTHOR

James P. Davis is associate professor at Denison University, where he teaches English and cultural studies.

CPSIA information can be obtained at www.ICGtesting.com
Printed in the USA
LVOW040133211211

260397LV00001B/3/P

9 781442 205697